Asynchronous Rust in Action:

A hands-on guide to building high-performance, scalable, and safe concurrent systems from the ground up.

By

Samuel E. Barnard

**Copyright © 2025 by
Samuel E. Barnard**

All rights reserved. No part of this publication may be reproduced, distributed, or transmitted in any form or by any means, including photocopying, recording, or other electronic or mechanical methods, without the prior written permission of the publisher, except in the case of brief quotations embodied in critical reviews and certain other noncommercial uses permitted by copyright law

Preface

In today's digital landscape, the demand for software that is both fast and massively scalable has never been higher. From real-time financial trading systems to social media platforms serving millions of concurrent users, the ability to handle thousands of operations at once is no longer a luxury—it's a requirement. Yet, traditional programming models often force us into a difficult trade-off: write simple, sequential code that struggles under load, or venture into the complex and bug-prone territory of multi-threaded programming.

This book is about a third, better way. It's about writing code that is incredibly fast, safe by default, and capable of handling immense concurrency with grace and clarity. This is the promise of asynchronous programming with the Rust language.

Asynchronous Rust represents a fundamental shift in how we build high-performance systems. It allows a single thread to juggle thousands of tasks efficiently, eliminating the performance bottlenecks of traditional I/O and the high overhead of massive thread pools. It's a technology that powers some of the world's most demanding applications, from the core infrastructure of cloud services to high-frequency trading desks.

But this book is not just about theory. It is a hands-on, practical guide designed to take you from the first principles of async to the final stages of deploying a production-ready application. We will journey together through a carefully structured path:

- First, we will build a solid understanding of *why* and *how* async works, demystifying concepts like async/await, Futures, and the role of an async runtime like Tokio.
- Next, we will master the essential tools of the trade, learning to manage state with concurrent data structures, communicate between tasks with channels, and handle errors gracefully in a parallel world.

- Then, we will put it all into practice by building a complete, high-performance, in-memory key-value store with a modern web API from the ground up.
- Finally, we will cover the crucial skills needed to take an application to production, including strategies for testing, debugging, monitoring, and packaging your service for deployment using Docker.

By the end of this book, you will not just understand asynchronous Rust; you will have the confidence and the skills to use it effectively. You will be equipped to build the next generation of safe, high-performance, and scalable concurrent systems from the ground up.

Table Of Contents

Chapter 1: 6

The 'Why' and 'How' of Asynchronous Rust.............................7

- Why Go Async? The Problem with Waiting 7
- The Asynchronous Mindset: Work Smarter, Not Harder 11
- Rust's Promise: Concurrency Without the Chaos 14
- Your First Async/Await Function.................................18
- The Runtime: The Engine That Drives Futures.............22

Chapter 2: 28

A Deep Dive into the Async Ecosystem 28

- A Deep Dive into the Async Ecosystem.......................28
- Working with Non-Blocking I/O: TCP and Files..........33
- Managing Time: Async Timers and Timeouts 39
- Spawning and Managing Concurrent Tasks 45
- The Problem with Standard `Mutex` in Async Code......50
- Limiting Concurrency with a `Semaphore` 56

Chapter 3: 60

Structuring Your Concurrent Applications 60

- Designing Applications with Concurrency in Mind 60
- Strategies for Graceful Error Handling in Concurrent Tasks 67
- Communicating Between Tasks Using Channels..........74
- Implementing the Actor Model for Better State Management..79
- Managing Shared Application State with `Arc<Mutex<T>>` 87

Chapter 4: 93

Advanced Async Techniques and Patterns 93
- Processing Continuous Data with the `Stream` Trait....93
- When and Why to Write Your Own `Future`: A Look at `Pin<T>` 97
- Integrating Blocking, Synchronous Code Without Freezing the Runtime 104
- Cancellation and Graceful Shutdown 110

Chapter 5: 116
Building a Real-World Application: A Concurrent Web Service...116
- Project Overview: A High-Performance Key-Value Store 116
- Implementing the Core Logic with Concurrent Data Structures 120
- Adding Layers: Middleware for Logging and Authentication 125
- Performance Tuning and Benchmarking 131

Chapter 6: 137
Testing, Debugging, and Deploying Async Rust.....................137
- Strategies for Testing Async Code 137
- Common Debugging Scenarios: Gaining Visibility with tracing 144
- Packaging Your Application for Production Using Docker...149
- Adding Monitoring and Observability with Prometheus Metrics 154
- A Look Toward the Future of Asynchronous Rust......160

Chapter 1:
The 'Why' and 'How' of Asynchronous Rust

Why Go Async? The Problem with Waiting

Imagine you're at a small coffee shop with a single, very methodical barista. You order a latte. The barista takes your order, grinds the beans, pulls the espresso shot, steams the milk, and finally, hands you your drink. While all this is happening—especially during the slow parts like the espresso machine brewing—the entire queue of people behind you just stands there, waiting. The barista is "blocked" on making your latte and can't even take the next person's order for a simple black coffee, which would have been much quicker to pour.

This is exactly how a basic computer program works. It executes instructions one after another. When it hits an instruction that involves waiting for something outside the CPU—like reading data from a hard drive, making a network request to another computer, or querying a database—it stops and waits. This is called **blocking I/O (Input/Output)**. The program's execution thread is completely frozen, just like the line at the coffee shop, until the slow operation is finished.

Let's look at what this means in code. Here's a simple, standard Rust program that reads the content of a file.

```rust
// A standard, synchronous way to read a file.
use std::fs;
use std::io;
use std::time::Instant;

fn main() -> io::Result<()> {
    let start = Instant::now();
    println!("Reading the file...");
```

```
    // This is a blocking call. The program will pause here.
    let content = fs::read_to_string("my_large_file.txt")?;

    println!("File read successfully! It took: {:?}", start.elapsed());
    println!("The first 100 characters are: '{}...'", &content[..100]);
    Ok(())
}
```

When the program executes fs::read_to_string, it sends a request to the operating system to fetch the file's contents from the disk. A modern processor can execute billions of instructions per second, but a physical disk drive is a mechanical device that is thousands of times slower. During that wait time, the thread running our program is effectively asleep. It's consuming memory and system resources but doing zero useful work. The CPU core assigned to it sits idle or gets switched to another process, which itself has a small performance cost (a "context switch").

For a simple command-line tool, this might not seem like a big deal. But what if this code was part of a web server?

The Snowball Effect in a Server
Let's scale up our coffee shop analogy. Now, it's a web server handling hundreds of user requests per second. Each request requires a "slow" database query that takes 100 milliseconds to complete.

If the server is written in a simple, synchronous style, it might handle requests like this:

1. A request comes in. Assign it to Thread 1.
2. Thread 1 processes the request and needs data from the database. It sends the query.
3. **Thread 1 is now blocked.** It sits and waits for the full 100ms for the database to respond. During this time, it cannot do anything else.

4. The database finally responds. Thread 1 wakes up, finishes processing, and sends the response to the user.
5. Only now is Thread 1 free to pick up a new incoming request.

If 10 requests arrive at the same time, the 10th user in line has to wait for the 9 previous requests to complete their 100ms database queries. Their total wait time will be nearly a full second, not because the server was working hard, but because it was spending most of its time just waiting.

The common solution to this is to throw more threads at the problem. If you have a pool of, say, 100 threads, you can handle 100 requests concurrently. But this approach doesn't scale well. Threads are not free; each one requires its own stack memory, and having the operating system manage hundreds or thousands of threads creates significant overhead. At some point, adding more threads makes the application slower, not faster.

Let's see this problem in a live code example. Here is a basic TCP server that accepts connections, but simulates a slow database query before responding.

```rust
use std::net::{TcpListener, TcpStream};
use std::io::{Read, Write};
use std::thread;
use std::time::Duration;

fn handle_client(mut stream: TcpStream) {
    println!("Handling client: {}", stream.peer_addr().unwrap());

    // Simulate a slow database query or other I/O work
    println!("Performing slow work for the client...");
    thread::sleep(Duration::from_secs(5));

    let response = "HTTP/1.1 200 OK\r\n\r\nHello from the slow server!";
```

```rust
        stream.write(response.as_bytes()).unwrap();
        stream.flush().unwrap();

        println!("Finished handling client.");
    }
}

fn main() -> std::io::Result<()> {
    let listener = TcpListener::bind("127.0.0.1:8080")?;
    println!("Server listening on port 8080");

    // This server handles clients one by one (sequentially).
    for stream in listener.incoming() {
        match stream {
            Ok(stream) => {
                // When a client connects, we handle them completely
                // before we can even accept another connection.
                handle_client(stream);
            }
            Err(e) => {
                eprintln!("Connection failed: {}", e);
            }
        }
    }
    Ok(())
}
```

If you run this code and try to connect with two browser tabs at once, you will notice the second tab won't even load until the first one has received its "Hello" message after 5 seconds. The listener.incoming() loop is blocked by handle_client.

This is the core performance problem that asynchronous programming solves. It offers a way to handle these waiting periods efficiently, allowing a single thread to manage thousands of concurrent tasks. Instead of the barista waiting for the espresso machine, they can take the next person's order, pour their simple black coffee, and then come back to the espresso machine once it's ready. This is the foundation of high-performance, scalable systems, and it's what we will build throughout this book.

The Asynchronous Mindset: Work Smarter, Not Harder

So, we've seen how a "blocking" approach brings our coffee shop to a grinding halt. How do we fix it? We don't necessarily need more baristas (threads). We need a smarter workflow.

Imagine a new, efficient barista. You order a latte. They take your order, start the espresso machine brewing—a process that takes a minute—and *immediately* turn to the next person in line. They take that person's order for a black coffee, pour it, and hand it over. Just then, the espresso machine beeps. The barista goes back, finishes your latte, and hands it to you.

Notice the difference? The barista never stood idle. While waiting for a slow operation (the brew), they switched to another task that was ready to be worked on. This is the essence of **non-blocking**, or asynchronous, programming.

When an application performs a non-blocking I/O operation, it doesn't wait for the result. It submits the request to the operating system and immediately moves on to other work. It essentially says, "Hey, start working on this file read for me, and just let me know when it's done."

The Role of the Runtime and the Event Loop

In this model, a part of your program called the **async runtime** acts as the manager. Its core component is an **event loop**. The event loop has a simple but critical job:

1. It maintains a list of tasks that are ready to do work.

2. It asks the operating system, "Have any of those slow I/O operations I gave you finished yet?" (e.g., "Is the data from that network socket available?").
3. If an operation is complete, the event loop takes the task that was waiting on it and puts it back in the "ready to work" list.
4. It picks a ready task and lets it run until it either finishes or hits another slow I/O operation, at which point the cycle repeats.

This single loop allows a single thread to juggle thousands of concurrent operations, keeping the CPU busy with tasks that are actually ready to make progress, instead of wasting cycles waiting.

Let's see how this looks conceptually in Rust with async/await.

```rust
// To run this, you need tokio in Cargo.toml:
// tokio = { version = "1", features = ["full"] }

use tokio::fs;

use std::time::Instant;

async fn read_files() {
    // Start reading the first file. When we .await, we yield control.
    // The runtime can start working on other tasks.
    let file1_future = fs::read_to_string("my_file1.txt");

    // Immediately start reading the second file, without waiting for the first.
    let file2_future = fs::read_to_string("my_file2.txt");
```

```rust
    // Now, we wait for both operations to complete. `tokio::join!`
    // waits for multiple futures concurrently. The runtime efficiently
    // handles the waiting for us.
    let (content1_result, content2_result) = tokio::join!(file1_future, file2_future);

    match content1_result {
        Ok(content) => println!("File 1 has {} characters.", content.len()),
        Err(e) => eprintln!("Error reading file 1: {}", e),
    }

    match content2_result {
        Ok(content) => println!("File 2 has {} characters.", content.len()),
        Err(e) => eprintln!("Error reading file 2: {}", e),
    }
}

#[tokio::main]
async fn main() {
    let start = Instant::now();
```

```
    read_files().await;

    println!("Total time elapsed: {:?}", start.elapsed());
}
```

In the synchronous world, we would have read the first file completely, then read the second, and the total time would be the sum of both reads. In this asynchronous example, tokio::join! allows the runtime to wait for both file reads *at the same time*. If each read takes 100ms, the total time will be roughly 100ms (plus a tiny bit of overhead), not 200ms.

This is the fundamental shift in thinking. We are no longer writing a linear sequence of steps but defining a set of tasks and the points where they can pause (.await), trusting the runtime to execute them as efficiently as possible. This is how we build systems that can handle a massive number of concurrent operations without breaking a sweat.

Rust's Promise: Concurrency Without the Chaos

We've seen that asynchronous programming is a powerful model for building efficient systems. But in many languages, writing concurrent code feels like walking a tightrope without a safety net. It's incredibly easy to make subtle mistakes that lead to maddeningly unpredictable bugs—bugs that only show up under heavy load in production. These are called **data races**.

A data race happens when multiple threads access the same memory location concurrently, at least one of the accesses is for writing, and there's no synchronization mechanism to control the accesses. The result is chaos. Your program's behavior becomes non-deterministic.

This is where Rust changes the game. It makes a bold promise: you can write fast, concurrent code without fear. This isn't just a marketing slogan; it's a guarantee enforced by the compiler.

Fearless Concurrency: Your Compiler as a Safety Net

The magic behind "fearless concurrency" is the same system that ensures memory safety in all Rust programs: the **ownership and borrow checking rules**. Before your code can even compile, the compiler rigorously analyzes how your program accesses data.

To put it simply:

1. **Ownership:** Every value in Rust has a single owner. When the owner goes out of scope, the value is dropped. This prevents memory leaks.
2. **Borrowing:** You can have either one mutable reference (`&mut T`) or any number of immutable references (`&T`) to a value, but not both at the same time.

The compiler extends these rules to a concurrent context using two special traits: `Send` and `Sync`.

- **Send**: A type is `Send` if it's safe to transfer ownership of its values to another thread. Most primitive types like `i32` and `String` are `Send`.
- **Sync**: A type is `Sync` if it's safe to have multiple threads access it via immutable references (`&T`) at the same time. If a type `T` is `Sync`, then `&T` is `Send`.

The compiler checks for these traits automatically. If you try to use a type across threads in a way that isn't safe, you don't get a runtime bug—you get a compile-time error.

Let's see this in action. Rust's `Rc<T>` (Reference Counted) pointer is used for shared ownership on a single thread. It is **not**

`Send`. Watch what happens when we try to send it to another thread:

```rust
use std::rc::Rc;
use std::thread;

fn main() {
    let data = Rc::new("some shared data");
    let data_clone = Rc::clone(&data);

    // This code will not compile!
    thread::spawn(move || {
        // The compiler stops us here.
        println!("Data from another thread: {}", data_clone);
    });

    println!("Data from main thread: {}", data);
}
```

If you try to compile this, you will get a clear error message:

```
error[E0277]: `Rc<&str>` cannot be sent safely between threads
  --> src/main.rs:8:5
   |
8  |     thread::spawn(move || {
   |     ^^^^^^^^^^^^^ `Rc<&str>` cannot be sent safely between threads
```

The compiler is our safety net. It has just prevented a potential data race. To share data across threads, Rust guides you to use a thread-safe equivalent like `Arc<T>` (Atomically Reference Counted), which is designed for this exact purpose. You don't have to guess; the compiler forces you to be correct.

Zero-Cost Abstractions: High-Level Code, Low-Level Speed

The second part of Rust's promise is performance. An "abstraction" is a high-level feature that hides complex details. In many languages, abstractions have a runtime cost—a garbage collector, a virtual machine, etc.

Rust's philosophy is **zero-cost abstractions**: the high-level features you use should compile down to machine code that is just as fast as if you had written the low-level equivalent by hand.

`async/await` is a perfect example of this principle. When you write an `async fn`, you're using a clean, high-level abstraction.

```rust
async fn process_data() {
    let data = read_from_network().await;
    let result = calculate(data);
    write_to_database(result).await;
}
```

Behind the scenes, the Rust compiler performs a remarkable transformation. It converts your `async` function into a highly efficient, self-contained **state machine**. This state machine is just a `struct` that holds all the state necessary for the function to run. Every `.await` point represents a possible state where the function can pause.

When you call `process_data()`, you don't actually run it. You get back this state machine object (a type that implements the `Future` trait). The async runtime then polls this future. If it's waiting on I/O, it gets put aside. When the I/O is ready, the runtime polls it again, and it continues executing from exactly where it left off, with all its local variables intact.

This entire process happens at compile time. The generated code is a lean, optimized state machine with no extra runtime overhead. You get the readability of `async/await` with the performance of meticulously hand-crafted, callback-based code.

Together, fearless concurrency and zero-cost abstractions mean you can write concurrent systems that are both safe by default and incredibly fast. You can focus on your application's logic, confident that the compiler will catch concurrency errors and generate highly efficient machine code.

Your First Async/Await Function

So far, we've talked a lot about the "why" of asynchronous programming. Now it's time to get our hands dirty and write some code. The `async` and `await` keywords are the heart of writing asynchronous Rust, and they are surprisingly simple to get started with.

The `async` Keyword: A Function That Can Pause

Think of the `async` keyword as a label you put on a function. This label changes a fundamental property of the function: it gives it the ability to be paused in the middle of its execution and resumed later.

A standard Rust function, once called, runs to completion without interruption. An `async` function, on the other hand, can willingly give up control when it encounters a potentially long-running operation.

Let's start with the simplest `async` function possible:

```rust
// This is an asynchronous function.
// It doesn't do much yet, but it has the special `async` property.
async fn our_first_async_function() {
    println!("Hello from inside an async function!");
}
```

That's it. Syntactically, the only difference is the `async` keyword before `fn`. But what happens when you try to call it like a regular function?

```rust
// This code won't do what you might expect.
fn main() {
```

```
    println!("Calling the async function...");
    our_first_async_function();
    println!("...or did we?");
}
```

If you run this, the output will be:

```
Calling the async function...
...or did we?
warning: call to `async` function
`our_first_async_function` is not awaited
```

Notice that "Hello from inside an async function!" is never printed. Instead, the compiler gives us a helpful warning. This is a critical concept: calling an `async` function does not run it. Instead, it creates and returns a value that represents the *potential* for that work to be done. This value is called a **Future**.

Think of a `Future` as a recipe. The recipe itself isn't a meal. It's a set of instructions that you can give to a chef (the async runtime) to prepare the meal for you later. Our `our_first_async_function()` call created the recipe, but we never hired a chef to cook it.

The `.await` Keyword: Pausing for the Result

This brings us to the `await` keyword. You use `.await` to take a `Future` and pause the current function's execution until that `Future` has completed. It's how you tell the "chef" to go ahead and start cooking and that you'll wait for the result before moving on.

You can only use `.await` from within another `async` function. Let's create a second function to call our first one.

```
async fn our_first_async_function() {
```

```rust
    println!("Hello from inside an async function!");
}

async fn run_our_functions() {

    println!("About to await our first function...");

    // .await will pause run_our_functions() and execute
    // our_first_async_function to completion.

    our_first_async_function().await;

    println!("Our first function has completed.");
}
```

This looks more complete, but we still have the same root problem: how do we start the "outermost" async function, `run_our_functions`? Our main function isn't async, so it can't use .await. We still need to hire the chef.

The Runtime: The Engine That Drives Futures

This is where an **async runtime** comes in. The runtime is the library that contains the "chef"—the **executor**—and all the other kitchen appliances. The executor's job is to take a top-level Future and run it until it's complete, managing all the pausing and resuming along the way.

tokio is the most popular async runtime in the Rust ecosystem. It provides a simple macro, #[tokio::main], that magically transforms our normal main function into an async entry point for our entire program. It sets up the executor and hands it our Future to run.

Let's put all the pieces together into a complete, working program.

First, you need to add `tokio` to your project's dependencies in your `Cargo.toml` file:

[dependencies]

tokio = { version = "1", features = ["full"] }

Now, we can write our final code:

```rust
use std::time::Duration;

// An async function that simulates some "work".
async fn our_first_async_function() {
    println!("-> Entering our_first_async_function.");
    // tokio::time::sleep is an async-aware pause.
    // It yields control back to the executor instead of blocking the thread.
    tokio::time::sleep(Duration::from_secs(1)).await;
    println!("<- Exiting our_first_async_function.");
}

// Another async function that calls the first one.
async fn run_our_functions() {
    println!("  -> Entering run_our_functions.");
    our_first_async_function().await;
    println!("  <- Exiting run_our_functions.");
}

// The tokio::main macro sets up the async runtime.
#[tokio::main]
async fn main() {
    println!("---> Program starting.");
    run_our_functions().await;
    println!("<--- Program finished.");
}
```

When you run this program, you will see the output appear in a specific, ordered sequence, with a one-second pause in the middle. The #[tokio::main] macro creates the runtime, which then executes the main function. When main awaits run_our_functions, it pauses and gives control to that function. And when run_our_functions awaits our_first_async_function, it does the same. Finally, tokio::time::sleep(...).await pauses for a second without blocking the entire system (the runtime would be free to run other tasks if we had any).

You have now successfully written and executed your first piece of asynchronous Rust code. You've learned the three core components:

1. **async fn**: Creates a function that can be paused, returning a Future.
2. **.await**: Pauses the current function to wait for a Future to complete.
3. **The Runtime (tokio)**: The engine that actually executes the Futures.

The Runtime: The Engine That Drives Futures

We've established that calling an async function creates a Future—a recipe for a task—but doesn't actually run it. You can .await a Future inside another async function, but this just nests the recipes. At the very top, something has to take that final recipe and start the cooking process. That "something" is the async runtime.

Think of the runtime as the entire kitchen staff and facility for our "chef" analogy. It's not just the chef (the **executor**) who runs the recipes; it's also the well-stocked pantry (I/O drivers), the timers on the ovens, and the system for passing orders around. tokio is the most widely-used, battle-tested runtime for building high-performance applications in Rust.

The Magic of #[tokio::main]

In our first complete example, we used #[tokio::main] to kick everything off. This attribute is a procedural macro, a powerful Rust feature that writes code for you at compile time. When you attach it to your main function, it does two key things:

1. It allows main to be an async fn.
2. It injects the code needed to build a new tokio runtime instance, take the Future that your async main function returns, and hand it to the runtime's executor to be run to completion.

Let's look at what the macro is doing for us conceptually. Our clean code:

```rust
#[tokio::main]

async fn main() {

    println!("Hello from async main!");

}
```

Is transformed by the compiler into something that looks roughly like this:

```rust
fn main() {

    // 1. Build a new Tokio runtime with default settings.

    let runtime = tokio::runtime::Builder::new_multi_thread()

        .enable_all()

        .build()

        .unwrap();
```

```rust
    // 2. Define the async logic inside a block.
    let future = async {
        println!("Hello from async main!");
    };

    // 3. Give the future to the runtime to execute.
    //    `block_on` will block the main thread until the future is complete.
    runtime.block_on(future);
}
```

The #[tokio::main] macro is a huge convenience, abstracting away the boilerplate of setting up and starting the runtime. This lets us focus on our application's logic right away.

More Than Just an Executor
A common misconception is that a runtime only executes Futures. tokio's power comes from being a complete platform for asynchronous I/O. Besides its world-class scheduler, it provides:

Asynchronous I/O Drivers: Non-blocking APIs for networking (TCP, UDP), file system operations, and standard input/output. When you use tokio::net::TcpStream or tokio::fs::File, you're using tokio's I/O drivers, which integrate directly with the operating system's most efficient event notification systems (like epoll on Linux or iocp on Windows).

Timers: A high-resolution timer for tasks that need to run after a specific duration or at a set interval. We've already seen tokio::time::sleep.

Synchronization Primitives: Thread-safe, async-aware versions of Mutex, Semaphore, RwLock, and channels (mpsc, oneshot, etc.) that know how to work with the runtime. When a task tries to acquire a lock that's already held, the runtime will suspend the task and wake it up only when the lock is released, rather than wastefully spinning the CPU.

Let's see this in a more practical example that uses a few of tokio's features. We'll spawn two tasks that run concurrently, managed entirely by the tokio runtime.

First, ensure your Cargo.toml enables the features we need:

```
[dependencies]
tokio = { version = "1", features = ["full"] }
```

Now, the code:

```
use tokio::time::{self, Duration};
use tokio::net::TcpListener;

// This task will simulate listening for database updates every 2 seconds.
async fn database_listener() {
    println!("[DB Task] Starting to listen for updates.");
    let mut interval = time::interval(Duration::from_secs(2));
    for i in 1..=3 {
        interval.tick().await; // This waits for the next tick in the interval.
        println!("[DB Task] Received update #{}.", i);
    }
    println!("[DB Task] Finished.");
}

// This task will accept incoming network connections.
async fn network_listener() {
    println!("[Net Task] Starting network listener on 127.0.0.1:8080");
```

```rust
    let listener = TcpListener::bind("127.0.0.1:8080").await.unwrap();

    // Accept one connection and then finish.
    match listener.accept().await {
        Ok((_socket, addr)) => println!("[Net Task] Accepted new connection from: {}", addr),
        Err(e) => eprintln!("[Net Task] Couldn't accept connection: {:?}", e),
    }
    println!("[Net Task] Finished.");
}

#[tokio::main]
async fn main() {
    println!("[Main] Spawning tasks...");

    // `tokio::spawn` hands a future to the runtime to be executed
    // concurrently in the background.
    let db_handle = tokio::spawn(database_listener());
    let net_handle = tokio::spawn(network_listener());

    println!("[Main] Tasks have been spawned. Main can do other work or wait.");

    // We use .await here to wait for both tasks to complete before the
    // program exits. `tokio::join!` is another way to do this.
    let _ = db_handle.await;
    let _ = net_handle.await;

    println!("[Main] All tasks have completed.");
}
```

When you run this program, you will see output from both tasks interleaved. The `tokio` runtime is intelligently switching between them. While the database task is sleeping for two seconds, the runtime can poll the network task to see if a connection has arrived. This is the power of the runtime in action: managing multiple independent, concurrent tasks and making sure no time is wasted waiting.

Chapter 2:
A Deep Dive into the Async Ecosystem

A Deep Dive into the Async Ecosystem

Welcome to the engine room. In the last chapter, we got our first taste of `async/await` and used the `#[tokio::main]` macro to get things running. It felt simple, almost magical. Now, we're going to pull back the curtain on that magic. This chapter is all about the **async runtime**, the powerful engine that drives our concurrent code. Understanding what the runtime is and what it does for you is the key to moving from writing simple async scripts to building robust, high-performance applications.

2.1 What is an Async Runtime, Really?

We've established that an `async` function returns a `Future`, which is an inert, lazy computation. It's a blueprint for work, not the work itself. The async runtime is the execution environment that takes these blueprints and brings them to life.

Think of it as a highly efficient, self-contained operating system living inside your Rust application, dedicated solely to managing your asynchronous tasks. It's a coordinated system composed of three critical parts:

1. **The Executor (or Scheduler):** The task manager that decides which task to run at any given moment.
2. **The I/O Driver (or Reactor):** The communications hub that handles all interaction with the operating system's I/O facilities (networking, files, etc.).
3. **The Timer:** The precise timing system that manages tasks needing to be woken up in the future.

When you use `#[tokio::main]`, you're getting a complete runtime with all three components, configured with sensible, production-ready defaults. Let's examine each component's role in detail.

The Executor: The Task Juggler

The most fundamental job of the runtime is to run `Future`s to completion. The component that does this is the **executor**. The executor maintains a collection of tasks that are ready to run. Its core operation is called **polling**. When the executor polls a `Future`, it's asking, "Can you make progress right now?" The `Future` must respond in one of two ways:

- `Poll::Ready(value)`: "Yes, I have finished my work, and here is the result." The executor can then move on.
- `Poll::Pending`: "No, I am currently waiting for something to happen (like data to arrive on the network). Please don't ask me again until you're notified that I'm ready."

When a `Future` returns `Pending`, a smart executor doesn't just wastefully ask it again and again. It puts the task to sleep and moves on to another one that is ready.

Tokio's Work-Stealing Scheduler

Tokio's default executor is a sophisticated **work-stealing scheduler**, which is exceptionally good at keeping multiple CPU cores busy. Here's how it works:

1. The runtime creates a pool of worker threads, typically one for each CPU core.
2. Each worker thread has its own local queue of tasks it's responsible for.
3. When a worker thread runs out of tasks in its own queue, it doesn't go to sleep. Instead, it looks at the queues of the

other worker threads and "steals" a task from the back of one of their queues.

This "stealing" is crucial for performance. It ensures that if one thread gets a batch of very short tasks and finishes quickly, it can immediately help out other threads that might be working on longer tasks. This load balancing keeps all CPU cores saturated with work, maximizing your application's throughput.

The I/O Driver: The Bridge to the World

This is where the true power of an async runtime shines, especially for network services. When your code awaits an I/O operation—like reading from a TCP socket—it's not the executor that waits. Instead, the task hands off responsibility to the **I/O driver** (also known as a **reactor**).

The driver's job is to be the single point of contact with the operating system's most efficient I/O notification system (`epoll` on Linux, `kqueue` on macOS/BSD, `IOCP` on Windows).

Let's trace the exact lifecycle of a single `socket.read().await` call. This detailed sequence is the heart of non-blocking I/O:

1. **Execution:** Your task is running on a worker thread. It reaches `socket.read(&mut buf).await`.
2. **First Poll:** The executor polls the `read` future. The future attempts to read from the socket. If no data is available from the OS, it cannot complete.
3. **Registration:** Instead of blocking, the future does two things:
    - It registers the socket with Tokio's I/O driver, telling it, "I am interested in knowing when this socket becomes readable."

- It gets a unique `Waker` object, which contains a "callback" that knows how to place this specific task back into the executor's ready queue. This `Waker` is stored alongside the socket registration.
4. **Suspend:** The future returns `Poll::Pending`. The executor sees this, suspends the task, and moves on to run other ready tasks. Your task is now "asleep" and consuming no CPU time.
5. **Waiting:** The I/O driver, on its own thread, is making a single, efficient call to the OS (e.g., `epoll_wait`), asking, "Let me know when anything happens on any of these hundreds of sockets I'm watching."
6. **Notification:** Data arrives on the network. The OS notifies the I/O driver that the socket is now readable.
7. **Waking Up:** The I/O driver looks up who was interested in this socket. It finds the stored `Waker` and calls its `wake()` method.
8. **Reschedule:** The `wake()` call places the sleeping task back into the executor's queue of runnable tasks.
9. **Second Poll:** At some point, a worker thread picks up your task again and polls its future. This time, when `socket.read()` is called, data is available. The read succeeds, the future returns `Poll::Ready(Ok(n))`, and your task continues execution from right after the `.await`.

This entire cycle happens thousands of times per second in a busy application, allowing a handful of threads to handle a massive number of I/O-bound connections concurrently.

The Timer: Managing Time Without Wasting It

Finally, the runtime provides a high-performance timer. When you call `tokio::time::sleep(duration).await`, you are not blocking a thread. You are registering a deadline with the runtime's timer.

The timer typically uses a highly efficient data structure (like a hierarchical timing wheel) to manage potentially thousands of pending timeouts without needing to scan a long list. It tells the runtime's core loop the time of the next closest deadline. The runtime can sleep until either an I/O event happens or the next timer is due. When a deadline is reached, the timer wakes the corresponding task, just like the I/O driver does.

This is extremely useful for implementing timeouts, a critical part of robust network programming. Let's see how the I/O driver and timer work together using `tokio::time::timeout`.

```rust
use tokio::io::AsyncReadExt;
use tokio::net::TcpStream;
use tokio::time::{self, Duration};

async fn process_socket(mut socket: TcpStream) {
    let mut buf = [0; 1024];

    // We'll wait a maximum of 5 seconds for the client to send us data.
    let timeout_duration = Duration::from_secs(5);

    // The `timeout` function wraps a future.
    match time::timeout(timeout_duration, socket.read(&mut buf)).await {
        // The inner future completed before the timeout.
        Ok(Ok(n)) => {
            println!("Read {} bytes: {}", n, String::from_utf8_lossy(&buf[..n]));
        }
        // The inner future returned an error.
        Ok(Err(e)) => {
            eprintln!("Socket read error: {}", e);
        }
        // The timeout elapsed.
        Err(_) => {
```

```
        eprintln!("Did not receive data within 5 seconds.");
      }
    }
}

#[tokio::main]
async fn main() {
    if let Ok(socket) = TcpStream::connect("127.0.0.1:8080").await {
        println!("Connected to server, will process socket.");
        process_socket(socket).await;
    } else {
        eprintln!("Failed to connect to server.");
    }
}
```

in this example, the `time::timeout` future coordinates with both the timer and the I/O driver. It asks the runtime to wake it up if *either* the socket becomes readable *or* 5 seconds have passed, whichever happens first. This is how you build resilient systems that don't wait forever on unreliable network clients.

Working with Non-Blocking I/O: TCP and Files

Input/Output (I/O) is the bread and butter of most network applications. It's the process of reading and writing data, whether from a network connection or a file on a disk. In an async context, performing these operations without blocking the executor is paramount. Tokio provides a suite of I/O tools in its `tokio::io`, `tokio::net`, and `tokio::fs` modules that integrate seamlessly with the runtime.

Network I/O: Building a TCP Server

Let's dive right into a practical example: a simple TCP server that accepts connections, reads a message from the client, converts it to uppercase, and sends it back. This "echo" server demonstrates the core concepts of asynchronous networking.

Tokio's networking primitives, like `TcpListener` and `TcpStream`, are designed to be non-blocking from the ground up.

- `tokio::net::TcpListener`: An async version of the standard library's listener. Its `accept()` method is an `async fn` that waits for a new connection without blocking the thread.
- `tokio::net::TcpStream`: Represents a connection between a client and a server. Its `read()` and `write()` methods are also `async` and are managed by the runtime's I/O driver.

Here is the full code for our uppercase echo server:

```rust
use tokio::io::{AsyncReadExt, AsyncWriteExt};

use tokio::net::TcpListener;

// To run this:

// 1. `cargo run`

// 2. In a separate terminal: `telnet 127.0.0.1 8080`

// 3. Type a message and press Enter.

#[tokio::main]

async fn main() -> std::io::Result<()> {

    // 1. Create the listener.

    let listener = TcpListener::bind("127.0.0.1:8080").await?;

    println!("Uppercase Echo Server listening on 127.0.0.1:8080");
```

```rust
    // 2. The main server loop.
    loop {
        // The .await here is crucial. The task pauses at this point,
        // allowing other tasks to run until a new connection arrives.
        let (mut socket, addr) = listener.accept().await?;
        println!("Accepted new connection from: {}", addr);

        // 3. Spawn a new task for each connection.
        // This allows the server to handle multiple clients concurrently.
        tokio::spawn(async move {
            let mut buf = vec![0; 1024];

            // 4. The connection's own loop.
            loop {
                // The .await here pauses this specific client's task
                // until data is received on its socket.
                match socket.read(&mut buf).await {
                    // Return value of `Ok(0)` means the client has closed the connection.
                    Ok(0) => {
                        println!("Connection closed by {}", addr);
```

```rust
                return;
            }
        Ok(n) => {
            // Convert the received data to uppercase.
            let received = &buf[..n];
            println!("Received {} bytes from {}", n, addr);
            let uppercased = received.to_ascii_uppercase();
            // The .await here pauses while writing the response back.
            if socket.write_all(&uppercased).await.is_err() {
                // If we can't write, the connection is likely broken.
                eprintln!("Failed to write to socket for {}", addr);
                return;
            }
        }
        Err(e) => {
            eprintln!("Failed to read from socket for {}: {}", addr, e);
            return;
```

```
            }
          }
        }
      });
    }
  }
}
```

Let's break down what's happening at each await point:
1. **`listener.accept().await`**: The main server task waits here. The `TcpListener` is registered with the I/O driver. The main task goes to sleep. When a client tries to connect, the OS notifies the driver, which wakes up the main task. The `accept` call completes, and the task proceeds.
2. **`tokio::spawn`**: We hand off the handling of the new connection to a completely new, independent task. This is vital. It allows our main loop to immediately go back to `listener.accept().await` to be ready for the *next* client, ensuring the server remains responsive.
3. **`socket.read(&mut buf).await`**: Inside the spawned task, we hit another await point. This client's task now goes to sleep, waiting for the user to send data. Importantly, this *only* pauses the task for this one client. If a hundred other clients are connected, their tasks can all be making progress while this one sleeps.
4. **`socket.write_all(&uppercased).await`**: Similarly, writing back to the socket is an async operation. The task yields control while the I/O driver manages sending the data over the network.

File I/O: A Different Kind of Asynchrony

Working with files from an async context presents a different challenge. On many operating systems, standard file APIs are fundamentally blocking. Unlike network sockets, there isn't always an efficient, event-based system like `epoll` for disk I/O. If you were to call a standard blocking file function from an async task, you would freeze the entire worker thread, preventing it from polling any other tasks. This is called "blocking the executor," and it's one of the primary things to avoid in async programming.

So how does Tokio solve this? Instead of trying to make file I/O non-blocking at the OS level, it uses a clever strategy: **it runs file operations on a separate, dedicated thread pool**. When you call an async file method like `tokio::fs::read`, Tokio takes your request, sends it to a background thread that is allowed to block, and your async task yields. Once the blocking file operation is complete on the background thread, it signals the main runtime, which then wakes up your original task to continue its work.

This gives you the ergonomic benefit of `async/await` while safely isolating the blocking behavior from your main, performance-critical async scheduler.

Let's see how to asynchronously read a file's contents.

```
use tokio::fs;

use tokio::io::AsyncReadExt;

// This example requires a file named `my_data.txt` in the same directory.

// Create it with some sample text.

#[tokio::main]

async fn main() -> std::io::Result<()> {

    println!("Attempting to read 'my_data.txt' asynchronously...");
```

```rust
// 1. Open the file asynchronously.

// This looks async, but under the hood, Tokio may use its blocking thread pool.

let mut file = fs::File::open("my_data.txt").await?;

// 2. Read the entire file content into a string.

let mut contents = String::new();

file.read_to_string(&mut contents).await?;

println!("File read successfully!");

println!("--- File Content ---");

println!("{}", contents);

println!("--------------------");

Ok(())
}
```

The programming model feels identical to the TCP example, even though the underlying mechanics are different. This is the power of a well-designed async runtime: it provides a consistent, high-level API while choosing the best implementation strategy for the task at hand. You, the developer, can simply `await` the result without needing to worry about whether it's being handled by the I/O driver or a blocking thread pool.

Managing Time: Async Timers and Timeouts

In programming, waiting isn't just about I/O. Often, you need to pause your code for a specific duration or stop an operation if it takes too long. Handling time is a fundamental part of building robust applications. A service that waits forever for a response from another system is a brittle service.

Just like with I/O, handling time in an async context requires special tools. A simple call to std::thread::sleep() would be disastrous, as it blocks the entire worker thread, bringing a chunk of your concurrent application to a standstill. Tokio provides a powerful and efficient time module, tokio::time, that integrates directly with the runtime's scheduler.

The Simplest Wait: tokio::time::sleep

The most basic time-related operation is pausing execution for a set duration. tokio::time::sleep is the asynchronous equivalent of std::thread::sleep. When you await a sleep, the function returns a Future that registers a deadline with the runtime's timer. The runtime then suspends your task and is free to work on other things. Once the specified duration has elapsed, the runtime's timer wakes your task up, and it continues execution.

```rust
use tokio::time::{sleep, Duration};
use std::time::Instant;

#[tokio::main]
async fn main() {
    let start = Instant::now();
    println!("Starting a task that will sleep.");

    // This creates a Future that will complete in 2 seconds.
    // The await pauses the main task, but not the whole thread.
    sleep(Duration::from_secs(2)).await;

    println!("Sleep finished after {:?}", start.elapsed());
}
```

This is the correct way to introduce a delay in an async function without blocking the executor.

Periodic Tasks: `tokio::time::interval`

Sometimes, you need to run a piece of code repeatedly at a fixed rate, like performing a health check every 30 seconds or polling a resource for updates. An `interval` is the perfect tool for this. It creates a stream that yields a value at a specified period.

Let's write a simple background task that "pings" a service every second for five seconds.

```rust
use tokio::time::{self, Duration};

async fn run_health_checks() {

    // Create an interval that ticks every 1 second.

    let mut interval = time::interval(Duration::from_secs(1));

    for i in 1..=5 {

        // The first tick completes immediately. Subsequent ticks will wait.

        interval.tick().await;

        println!("Performing health check #{}...", i);

        // In a real app, you would perform the actual health check logic here.

    }

    println!("Finished health checks.");

}

#[tokio::main]

async fn main() {
```

```
tokio::spawn(run_health_checks()).await.unwrap();
}
```

The `.tick().await` call will pause the task until the next second has passed, making it an efficient way to build background tasks and cron jobs within your application.

The Essential Tool for Robustness: `tokio::time::timeout`

This is one of the most important functions in the async toolkit. In a distributed system, you cannot guarantee that a remote service will respond in a timely manner, or at all. If you `await` a future that depends on a network response, your task could hang forever if the remote end never replies. This is a common source of bugs and cascading failures.

`tokio::time::timeout` wraps another `Future` and gives it a deadline. It returns a `Result`.

- If the inner `Future` completes before the timeout, `timeout` returns `Ok(result)`.
- If the timeout elapses before the inner `Future` completes, `timeout` returns `Err(Elapsed)`.

This allows you to gracefully handle slow or unresponsive operations. Let's modify our TCP client logic to include a timeout. Imagine we are connecting to a service that is sometimes slow. We don't want to wait more than 2 seconds for a response.

```
use tokio::net::TcpStream;

use tokio::io::AsyncReadExt;

use tokio::time::{self, Duration};
```

```rust
async fn get_data_from_slow_service() -> std::io::Result<Vec<u8>> {
    println!("Connecting to the slow service...");
    // Let's pretend this is a service that sometimes takes too long.
    // To test this, you can use the echo server from the previous section
    // and just not send any data from the telnet client.
    let mut stream = TcpStream::connect("127.0.0.1:8080").await?;
    println!("Connected. Waiting for data...");
    let mut buffer = Vec::new();
    stream.read_to_end(&mut buffer).await?;
    Ok(buffer)
}

#[tokio::main]
async fn main() {
    let timeout_duration = Duration::from_secs(2);
    println!("Calling service with a {}s timeout.", timeout_duration.as_secs());


    match time::timeout(timeout_duration, get_data_from_slow_service()).await {
```

```
    // The outer Ok means the timeout function itself completed.

    // The inner Ok means our `get_data_from_slow_service`
completed successfully.

    Ok(Ok(data)) => {

        println!("Received data successfully: {} bytes.", data.len());

    }

    // The inner Err means our function failed with a standard I/O error.

    Ok(Err(e)) => {

        eprintln!("Service returned an error: {}", e);

    }

    // The outer Err means the timeout was triggered.

    Err(_) => {

        eprintln!("Error: Timed out waiting for the service to respond.");

    }

    }

}
```

By wrapping the call in `timeout`, we've made our application more resilient. It now has a predictable failure mode instead of an unpredictable hang. Using timeouts for all I/O operations that can fail or stall is a critical best practice for writing production-grade, reliable systems.

Spawning and Managing Concurrent Tasks

So far, we've seen how `async/await` allows a single task to pause and resume, enabling other work to happen. But the real power of a runtime like Tokio is its ability to run many independent tasks at the same time. This is where `tokio::spawn` comes in. It is the primary tool for creating true, background concurrency.

When you `await` a future directly, you are using **structured concurrency**. The awaited future must complete before the parent function can continue. `tokio::spawn`, on the other hand, breaks this structure. It takes a future and hands it off to the Tokio scheduler to be run as a new, top-level task in the background. The original task that called `spawn` doesn't wait; it continues executing its own code immediately.

This lets you fire-and-forget background tasks, build systems with multiple independent components, and process many units of work in parallel.

Your First Spawned Task

Let's see the difference between `await` and `spawn` with a simple example.

```
use tokio::time::{self, Duration};

// A simple async function that simulates some work.
async fn say_hello_from_task() {
    // This task will wait for 1 second.
    time::sleep(Duration::from_secs(1)).await;
    println!("Hello from the spawned task!");
}

#[tokio::main]
async fn main() {
```

```rust
    println!("Spawning a new task...");

    // `tokio::spawn` immediately returns a `JoinHandle`.
    // The original task does not wait for the spawned task to complete.
    let handle = tokio::spawn(say_hello_from_task());

    // The main task continues its execution right away.
    println!("Spawned task is running in the background. Main task continues.");

    // We can do other work here...
    time::sleep(Duration::from_millis(100)).await;

    println!("Main task is about to finish.");
    // If main finishes, the program might exit before the spawned task prints its message.
    // To prevent this, we can wait on the handle.
    // The .await here will pause main until the spawned task is complete.
    // The outer `unwrap` handles potential panics in the spawned task.
    handle.await.unwrap();
    println!("Main task has waited for the spawned task to complete.");
}
```

When you run this, you'll see the output from `main` appear immediately, and then, after about a second, the message from the spawned task will print.

The `JoinHandle`: Your Handle on the Task

When you `spawn` a task, Tokio gives you back a `JoinHandle`. This handle is your connection to the background task. It serves two main purposes:

1. **Waiting for Completion**: As seen in the example, you can `.await` the handle to pause the current task until the spawned task finishes. This is how you "join" the background task back into your main flow of execution.
2. **Getting a Result**: If the spawned `async` block returns a value, you can retrieve it from the `JoinHandle` after awaiting it. The result is wrapped in a `Result` because a spawned task could panic, which the `JoinHandle` will catch and report as an `Err`.

Here's how to get a value back from a spawned task:

```rust
use tokio::time::{self, Duration};

async fn calculate_complex_value() -> i32 {

    time::sleep(Duration::from_secs(1)).await;

    42 // The return value of our calculation.

}

#[tokio::main]

async fn main() {

    let handle = tokio::spawn(calculate_complex_value());

    // Do other work...

    println!("Doing other work while the calculation runs...");

    // Wait for the handle and get the result.

    // The `await` returns a `Result<i32, JoinError>`.

    match handle.await {
```

```rust
        Ok(value) => {
            println!("The spawned task calculated the value: {}", value);
        }
        Err(e) => {
            eprintln!("The spawned task panicked: {}", e);
        }
    }
}
```

Managing Multiple Tasks

The real power of `spawn` becomes apparent when you create many tasks. A common pattern is to loop through a collection of work items, spawn a task for each one, collect the handles, and then wait for them all to complete.

This pattern is perfect for parallelizing work, such as making multiple network requests simultaneously.

```rust
use tokio::time::{self, Duration};

// A function that simulates a network request to fetch a user.
async fn fetch_user(id: i32) -> String {
    // Simulate network latency.
    time::sleep(Duration::from_millis(500)).await;
    println!("Fetched user {}", id);
    format!("User-{}", id)
```

}

#[tokio::main]

async fn main() {

   let mut handles = vec![];

   println!("Spawning tasks to fetch 5 users in parallel.");

   for i in 1..=5 {

      // For each user ID, we spawn a new task.

      let handle = tokio::spawn(fetch_user(i));

      // We store the handle to wait on it later.

      handles.push(handle);

   }

   // Now we have 5 tasks running concurrently in the background.

   // We can wait for them all to finish.

   let mut results = vec![];

   for handle in handles {

      // `await` each handle to get the result of that task.

      results.push(handle.await.unwrap());

   }

```
    println!("\nAll tasks completed!");

    println!("Fetched data: {:?}", results);
}
```

Even though each `fetch_user` call takes 500ms, the entire process will take just a little over 500ms (not 2.5 seconds) because all five tasks run concurrently. Tokio's scheduler distributes them across the available CPU cores, and while they are "sleeping," they consume no CPU time at all. This is the foundation of building high-throughput, parallel systems in Rust.

The Problem with Standard Mutex *in Async Code*

Rust's standard library provides `std::sync::Mutex`. It's a perfectly good `Mutex` for multi-threaded programming. When a thread tries to acquire a lock that's already held, `std::sync::Mutex` **blocks the thread**. It simply freezes that thread until the lock becomes available.

As we've learned, blocking a worker thread in an async runtime is catastrophic. It prevents the thread's executor from polling any of the other tasks it's managing, causing stalls and massive performance degradation.

The Async Solution: `tokio::sync::Mutex`

This is why Tokio provides its own, async-aware `Mutex`: `tokio::sync::Mutex`. It's designed to work seamlessly with the async runtime. When you try to acquire a lock that's already held, its `.lock()` method returns a future. When you `.await` this future:

- If the lock is available, your task acquires it and continues immediately.
- If the lock is held by another task, the runtime suspends your task and puts it to sleep. It does **not** block the thread.

When the lock is released, the runtime wakes up your task, which can then acquire the lock and continue.

Sharing a Mutex with `Arc`

A `Mutex` on its own can't be shared across multiple tasks because that would violate Rust's ownership rules. To share ownership of the `Mutex` itself, we need to wrap it in an `Arc` (Atomically Reference-Counted pointer). `Arc` allows multiple tasks to have a handle to the same data without a single owner.

The combination `Arc<Mutex<T>>` is the canonical way to share mutable state in async Rust. Let's see it in action with a shared counter.

```rust
use std::sync::Arc;

use tokio::sync::Mutex;

use tokio::time::{self, Duration};

#[tokio::main]

async fn main() {

    // 1. Wrap the data (our counter, a u32) in a Tokio Mutex.

    // 2. Wrap the Mutex in an Arc to allow shared ownership.

    let shared_counter = Arc::new(Mutex::new(0));

    let mut handles = vec![];

    println!("Spawning 10 tasks to increment a shared counter...");



    for i in 0..10 {
```

// Create a new Arc pointer for each task. This increases the reference count.

let counter_clone = Arc::clone(&shared_counter);

let handle = tokio::spawn(async move {

    // The .await here is the key. If the lock is held, this task will

    // yield control and sleep until the lock is available.

    let mut num = counter_clone.lock().await;

    // The lock is now held by this task.

    // Dereference `num` to get the underlying u32 and increment it.

    *num += 1;

    println!("Task {} incremented counter to: {}", i, *num);

    // The lock is automatically released when `num` (the MutexGuard) goes out of scope here.

});

handles.push(handle);

}

// Wait for all tasks to complete.

for handle in handles {

>   handle.await.unwrap();
>
>   }
>
>   // Lock one last time to read the final value.
>
>   let final_value = *shared_counter.lock().await;
>
>   println!("\nFinal counter value is: {}", final_value);
>
> }

When you run this, you'll see the tasks executing in a non-deterministic order, but the final count will always be 10. The `Mutex` successfully protected the shared `u32` from concurrent access.

For Read-Heavy Workloads: `RwLock`

A `Mutex` is simple, but it can be inefficient if your data is read far more often than it is written. A `Mutex` forces every operation to be exclusive; even if ten tasks just want to read the data, they have to line up and do it one by one.

This is where a **Read-Write Lock (`RwLock`)** is a better choice. `tokio::sync::RwLock` provides more granular locking with two modes:

- **A "read" lock**: Any number of tasks can acquire a read lock simultaneously.
- **A "write" lock**: Only one task can acquire a write lock. While it is held, no other tasks can acquire a read *or* a write lock.

This is perfect for data like a shared configuration cache that is read by many request handlers but only updated occasionally by a background task.

```rust
use std::collections::HashMap;
use std::sync::Arc;
use tokio::sync::RwLock;
use tokio::time::{self, Duration};
#[tokio::main]
async fn main() {
    let shared_config = Arc::new(RwLock::new(HashMap::from([
        ("server_name".to_string(), "Main Server".to_string()),
    ])));
    // Spawn a writer task to update the config after a delay.
    let writer_clone = Arc::clone(&shared_config);
    tokio::spawn(async move {
        time::sleep(Duration::from_millis(600)).await;
        println!("[Writer] Trying to acquire write lock...");
        // Acquire an exclusive write lock.
        let mut config = writer_clone.write().await;
        config.insert("server_name".to_string(), "Updated Server".to_string());
```

```rust
        println!("[Writer] Updated server name.");
        // Write lock is released here.
    });
    // Spawn multiple reader tasks.
    let mut reader_handles = vec![];
    for i in 0..5 {
        let reader_clone = Arc::clone(&shared_config);
        let handle = tokio::spawn(async move {
            // Readers will run concurrently at first.
            time::sleep(Duration::from_millis(i * 100)).await;
            println!("[Reader {}] Trying to acquire read lock...", i);
            // Acquire a shared read lock.
            let config = reader_clone.read().await;
            println!("[Reader {}] Server name is: '{}'", i, config.get("server_name").unwrap());
            // Read lock is released here.
        });
        reader_handles.push(handle);
```

```
    }
    for handle in reader_handles {
        handle.await.unwrap();
    }
}
```

In this example, the reader tasks can all acquire their locks and read the initial "Main Server" value. When the writer task wakes up and calls `.write().await`, it will wait for all existing readers to finish, then acquire its exclusive lock. Any new readers trying to acquire a lock while the writer is working will be put to sleep until the write lock is released.

Limiting Concurrency with a `Semaphore`

While a `Mutex` is essential for guaranteeing exclusive access to data, sometimes "only one at a time" is too restrictive. There are many scenarios where you want to allow a certain number of tasks to access a resource concurrently, but no more than that.

Imagine a web application that needs to connect to a database. Database servers can only handle a finite number of simultaneous connections. If your application gets a sudden spike in traffic and tries to open thousands of connections at once, you could overwhelm and crash the database. What you really want is a way to maintain a **pool** of, say, 10 active connections, and have any excess requests wait politely in line until a connection becomes free.

This is precisely the problem that a **Semaphore** solves. A semaphore is a synchronization primitive that maintains a set of permits. To access the protected resource, a task must first acquire a permit from the semaphore. If no permits are available, the task waits until another task releases one.

Mutex vs. Semaphore

- A `Mutex` is for **exclusive access**. It's fundamentally a semaphore with only **one** permit.
- A `Semaphore` is for **controlling concurrency levels**. It allows up to N tasks to proceed at the same time.

You can use a semaphore to control access to any resource with a limited capacity, such as:

- A database connection pool.
- The number of concurrent requests to a rate-limited third-party API.
- The number of CPU-intensive tasks running at once, to avoid overloading the system.

Using `tokio::sync::Semaphore`

Tokio's `Semaphore` works very similarly to its `Mutex`. You create it with a specific number of permits. The `acquire()` method is an async function that returns a future. When you `.await` it, your task will pause until a permit is available. The method returns a `SemaphorePermit`, which is a guard object. When this guard is dropped (goes out of scope), the permit is automatically returned to the semaphore for another task to use.

Let's build a simulation of an API client that needs to respect a rate limit. The external API only allows us to make 3 concurrent requests. We'll have 10 jobs that need to be done, and we'll use a semaphore to ensure we never exceed the API's limit.

```
use std::sync::Arc;
use tokio::sync::Semaphore;
use tokio::time::{self, Duration};

// This function simulates making a call to a rate-limited
external API.
```

```rust
async fn call_external_api(task_id: i32) {
    println!("[Task {}] Ready to make API call.", task_id);
    // Simulate the network call latency.
    time::sleep(Duration::from_secs(1)).await;
    println!("[Task {}] <<< API call complete.", task_id);
}

#[tokio::main]
async fn main() {
    // 1. Create a semaphore that will allow up to 3 concurrent tasks.
    let semaphore = Arc::new(Semaphore::new(3));
    let mut handles = vec![];

    println!("Spawning 10 tasks to call an API with a concurrency limit of 3.");

    for i in 0..10 {
        // We need to share the semaphore across tasks, so we clone the Arc.
        let semaphore_clone = Arc::clone(&semaphore);

        let handle = tokio::spawn(async move {
            // 2. Acquire a permit. The .await will pause this task if all 3
            //    permits are currently in use by other tasks.
            let permit = semaphore_clone.acquire().await.unwrap();
            println!("[Task {}] >>> Acquired permit. Concurrency: {}", i, 3 - semaphore_clone.available_permits());

            call_external_api(i).await;

            // 3. The permit is automatically released when `permit` goes out of scope here.
            //    Another waiting task can now acquire it.
            println!("[Task {}] --- Released permit.", i);
```

```
    });
    handles.push(handle);
}

for handle in handles {
    handle.await.unwrap();
}

println!("\nAll API calls have been completed.");
}
```

When you run this code, you'll see the output clearly demonstrates how the semaphore controls the flow:

1. The first three tasks (e.g., Task 0, 1, 2) will immediately acquire a permit and start their "API call."
2. The subsequent tasks (3 through 9) will be created, but when they try to acquire a permit, they will be suspended because the semaphore is at its capacity of 3.
3. As soon as one of the first three tasks completes its `sleep` and its `permit` guard is dropped, the semaphore has a free permit again.
4. The Tokio runtime will then wake up one of the waiting tasks (e.g., Task 3), which will then acquire the newly freed permit and begin its work.

This continues until all 10 tasks have had a chance to run. The semaphore gracefully queues the work, ensuring that we never violate the concurrency limit of our critical resource. This is a powerful and essential pattern for building robust, well-behaved systems.

Chapter 3:
Structuring Your Concurrent Applications

Designing Applications with Concurrency in Mind

Trying to add concurrency to an application that wasn't designed for it is like trying to add a second story to a house that was only built with a foundation for one. You can do it, but it's often awkward, expensive, and the result is less stable than if you had planned for it from the beginning.

True high-performance systems don't have concurrency bolted on as an afterthought; it's woven into their very structure. Thinking about concurrency from the start forces you to make better design decisions that lead to cleaner, more scalable, and more resilient code. Let's walk through the key principles of this design-first approach.

1. Identify Your Independent Units of Work

The very first step is to look at your application's purpose and break it down into logical, independent tasks. Ask yourself: "What operations can happen at the same time without interfering with each other?"

Consider a typical web server handling a request to view a user's profile page. A synchronous approach would be a linear sequence:

1. Receive request.
2. Authenticate the user's session token.
3. Query the database for the user's details.
4. Make an API call to a separate service to get the user's recent activity.
5. Make another API call to an ads service to get personalized ads.

6. Render the HTML page.
7. Send the response.

Now, let's look at this with a concurrency mindset. We can immediately see independent units of work:

- The database query for user details (Task A).
- The API call for recent activity (Task B).
- The API call for ads (Task C).

None of these three tasks depend on each other. A concurrent design would execute all three *in parallel*. Instead of waiting for A, then B, then C, we can `spawn` three separate tasks and wait for them all to complete. The total time spent waiting is only as long as the *slowest* of the three tasks, not the sum of all three.

```rust
use tokio::time::{self, Duration};

async fn get_user_details() -> String {

    // Simulate DB query

    time::sleep(Duration::from_millis(150)).await;

    "User Details".to_string()

}

async fn get_user_activity() -> String {

    // Simulate API call

    time::sleep(Duration::from_millis(200)).await;

    "User Activity".to_string()

}

async fn get_personalized_ads() -> String {
```

```rust
    // Simulate another API call
    time::sleep(Duration::from_millis(100)).await;
    "Personalized Ads".to_string()
}
#[tokio::main]
async fn main() {
    let start_time = time::Instant::now();
    // Spawn all three tasks to run concurrently.
    let user_details_handle = tokio::spawn(get_user_details());
    let user_activity_handle = tokio::spawn(get_user_activity());
    let ads_handle = tokio::spawn(get_personalized_ads());
    // Wait for all of them to complete using tokio::join!
    let (details, activity, ads) = tokio::join!(
        user_details_handle,
        user_activity_handle,
        ads_handle
    );
    println!("Fetched Data:");
println!("- {}", details.unwrap());
```

```
    println!("- {}", activity.unwrap());

    println!("- {}", ads.unwrap());

    println!("\nTotal time elapsed: {:?}", start_time.elapsed());
}
```

Running this code shows a total time of just over 200ms (the duration of the longest task), not the 450ms it would have taken sequentially. Identifying these parallel operations is the first and most impactful step in concurrent design.

2. Define Communication, Not Just Behavior

Once you have your tasks, you must define how they interact. A common mistake is to think only about what each task *does* and not how it *communicates*. The communication pattern is a core part of your architecture. You have two primary models:

- **Shared-State Concurrency (`Arc<Mutex<T>>`)**: Tasks communicate by accessing and modifying the same piece of shared memory. This is like a team of writers editing the same document directly. It's simple for small problems, but can lead to bottlenecks (contention) as many tasks wait to acquire the same lock.
- **Message-Passing Concurrency (Channels)**: Tasks are completely isolated and own all their own data. They communicate by sending messages to each other over channels. This is like writers sending emails with their changes to a single editor. It often leads to cleaner, more decoupled code that is easier to reason about.

A good design often prefers channels for high-level communication between major components and reserves shared-state mutexes for fine-grained data that truly must be shared.

3. Plan Your State Management

Closely related to communication is your strategy for managing state. Where does your application's data live?

- **Task-Local State**: This is the ideal. Each spawned task owns all the data it needs. There is no sharing, no locking, and no complexity. You should structure your code to maximize this wherever possible.
- **The Actor Model**: This is a powerful pattern for when state absolutely must be shared. Instead of spreading `Arc<Mutex<T>>` handles throughout your application, you encapsulate the state within a single, dedicated task (the "actor"). This actor listens on a channel for "commands" (messages). It is the only task allowed to modify the state directly. Other tasks communicate with it by sending command messages and, if necessary, waiting for a response. This centralizes state management and avoids deadlock scenarios, as the locking logic is contained entirely within the actor's implementation.

Here's a conceptual actor for managing a user's score:

```rust
use tokio::sync::{mpsc, oneshot};

// Commands that can be sent to our actor.
enum ScoreCommand {
    AddScore { amount: u32 },
    GetScore { responder: oneshot::Sender<u32> },
}

// The actor task itself.
async fn score_manager_actor(mut receiver: mpsc::Receiver<ScoreCommand>) {
    let mut score = 0;
    while let Some(command) = receiver.recv().await {
        match command {
            ScoreCommand::AddScore { amount } => {
```

```
            score += amount;
            println!("[Actor] Score is now {}", score);
        }
        ScoreCommand::GetScore { responder } => {
            // Send the current score back to the requester.
            let _ = responder.send(score);
        }
      }
    }
  }
}
```

// In main, you would spawn this actor and send it commands.
// This is a design pattern we will explore more deeply later.

Design for Shutdown

In a concurrent application, stopping gracefully is a feature you must design for, not an afterthought. What happens when you want to shut down your server? You can't just kill the process; you might interrupt a database write or leave a user's request half-finished.

A robust design includes a clear shutdown signal. A `tokio::sync::broadcast` channel is an excellent tool for this. You can create a "shutdown" channel and give a receiver to every long-running task. When it's time to shut down, you send a single message on this channel. Each task's main loop should be structured to listen for this signal and exit cleanly.

```rust
// A simplified shutdown mechanism
async fn long_running_task(id: u32, mut shutdown_rx: tokio::sync::broadcast::Receiver<()>) {
    loop {
        // tokio::select! lets a task wait on multiple futures at once.
        tokio::select! {
            // This branch runs if a shutdown signal is received.
            _ = shutdown_rx.recv() => {
                println!("[Task {}] Shutdown signal received. Exiting.", id);
                break;
            }
            // This is the task's normal work.
            _ = tokio::time::sleep(Duration::from_secs(1)) => {
                println!("[Task {}] Doing some work...", id);
            }
        }
    }
}
```

Thinking about these four areas—identifying work, defining communication, managing state, and planning for failure—from the very beginning will guide you toward building applications that are not just fast, but also clean, resilient, and ready to scale.

Strategies for Graceful Error Handling in Concurrent Tasks

In a single-threaded program, error handling is straightforward. A function returns a `Result`, and you either handle the `Err` variant immediately or propagate it up the call stack with the `?` operator.

But when you `tokio::spawn` a task, you create a new, independent execution context. If that task fails, what happens? By default, nothing. The task simply terminates. It won't crash your application, but it might silently stop doing its important work, leading to subtle, hard-to-diagnose bugs. A background task that's supposed to be processing payments could fail, and you might not know until customers start complaining.

Graceful error handling in a concurrent system means ensuring that failures are always detected, reported, and acted upon appropriately.

The First Line of Defense: The `JoinHandle`

As we've seen, `tokio::spawn` returns a `JoinHandle`. This handle is not just for getting a successful result back; it's also your primary mechanism for detecting failures in tasks that are expected to complete.

When you `.await` a `JoinHandle`, it doesn't just return the value that the task produced. It returns a `Result<T, JoinError>`, where `T` is the value returned by the task.

- **`Ok(T)`**: The task completed successfully, and `T` is its return value.
- **`Err(JoinError)`**: The task failed. A `JoinError` indicates that the task panicked.

Let's see how to check for a panic.

```rust
#[tokio::main]
async fn main() {
    let handle = tokio::spawn(async {
        println!("[Task] I'm about to panic!");
        panic!("Something went terribly wrong!");
    });
    // The main task continues, unaware of the panic for now.
    println!("[Main] Spawned a task that will panic.");
    // Now, we await the handle to check the task's outcome.
    match handle.await {
        Ok(_) => {
            println!("[Main] Task completed without panicking.");
        }
        Err(e) => {
            // The JoinError tells us the task panicked.
            if e.is_panic() {
                eprintln!("[Main] The spawned task panicked! Error: {:?}", e);
            }
        }
```

```
    }
}
```

Catching panics is a good safety net, but in most cases, your tasks shouldn't be panicking. They should be returning a `Result` to indicate a recoverable failure.

Propagating `Results` from Spawned Tasks

A much more common and structured way to handle errors is to have your async block return a `Result`. When you do this, the type `T` in the `JoinHandle`'s `Result<T, JoinError>` becomes a `Result` itself. This creates a nested `Result`: `Result<Result<SuccessType, ErrorType>, JoinError>`.

This might look complex, but it gives you complete information:

- `Ok(Ok(value))`: The task finished and returned a successful `Ok` value.
- `Ok(Err(error))`: The task finished and returned a recoverable `Err`.
- `Err(join_error)`: The task panicked and did not finish normally.

Here's a practical example of a task that tries to perform a fallible operation, like reading from a file that might not exist.

```
use std::io;

async fn read_important_file() -> io::Result<String> {

    // This will return Ok(contents) or Err(error).

    tokio::fs::read_to_string("config.toml").await

}
```

```rust
#[tokio::main]

async fn main() {

    let handle = tokio::spawn(read_important_file());

    println!("[Main] Waiting for file reading task to complete...");

    match handle.await {

        // Task panicked.

        Err(join_error) => {

            eprintln!("[Main] Task panicked: {}", join_error);

        }

        // Task finished, let's check its own Result.

        Ok(result_from_task) => {

            match result_from_task {

                Ok(contents) => {

                    println!("[Main] Task success! Contents: {:.20}...", contents);

                }

                Err(io_error) => {

                    eprintln!("[Main] Task failed with I/O error: {}", io_error);

                }
```

```
        }
      }
    }
}
```

This pattern is excellent for "work-to-completion" tasks where the main logic needs to know the precise outcome before proceeding.

A More Advanced Pattern: Error Reporting Channels

The `JoinHandle` approach works well when you're spawning a task and waiting for its result. But what about long-running, "always-on" background tasks, like our TCP echo server from the last chapter? You don't want to join that task; you want it to run forever. But you still need to know if it encounters an error.

For this, a powerful pattern is to use **channels**. You can create a central MPSC (multi-producer, single-consumer) channel dedicated to error reporting. Any spawned task can be given a clone of the channel's sender. If a task encounters an error, it doesn't terminate; it simply sends the error object down the channel and continues its work. A single, dedicated "error handling" task can then listen on the receiving end, logging or acting on errors from across the entire application.

This decouples error *occurrence* from error *handling*.

```
use tokio::sync::mpsc;

use std::io;

// A worker function that simulates doing work that can fail.

async fn worker_task(id: u32, error_tx: mpsc::Sender<String>) {

    loop {
```

```rust
        println!("[Worker {}] Doing some work...", id);

        tokio::time::sleep(tokio::time::Duration::from_secs(id as u64 + 1)).await;

        // Simulate a random failure.
        if rand::random::<bool>() {
            let error_message = format!("[Worker {}] Encountered a critical failure!", id);

            println!("{}", error_message);

            // Send the error to the central handler.
            if error_tx.send(error_message).await.is_err() {
                // If the channel is closed, we can't report errors, so we stop.
                eprintln!("[Worker {}] Error channel closed. Shutting down.", id);

                break;
            }
        } else {
            println!("[Worker {}] Work completed successfully.", id);
        }
    }
}
```

```rust
#[tokio::main]
async fn main() {
    // 1. Create a channel for error reporting.
    let (error_tx, mut error_rx) = mpsc::channel(100);

    // 2. Spawn a dedicated error handling task.
    let error_handler = tokio::spawn(async move {
        println!("[Error Handler] Started.");
        // This loop will run as long as there are active senders.
        while let Some(error_msg) = error_rx.recv().await {
            eprintln!("[Error Handler] Received error: {}", error_msg);
            // Here you could add logic to restart tasks, send alerts, etc.
        }
        println!("[Error Handler] Shutting down.");
    });

    // 3. Spawn multiple worker tasks, giving each a clone of the sender.
    for i in 1..=3 {
        let tx_clone = error_tx.clone();
```

```
        tokio::spawn(worker_task(i, tx_clone));
}

    // Drop the original sender so the error handler's `recv` loop
    // will eventually end when all worker tasks have finished.
    drop(error_tx);
    // Wait for the error handler to finish. In a real server,
    // this might run forever or until a shutdown signal.
    error_handler.await.unwrap();
}
```

This channel-based approach is extremely flexible and is a cornerstone of building resilient, long-running services. It allows you to centralize your error logging and response logic, making your application much cleaner and easier to manage.

Communicating Between Tasks Using Channels

In any system with more than one concurrent task, you inevitably face a critical design choice: how will these tasks talk to each other? Broadly, there are two main approaches:

1. **Shared-State Concurrency**: Tasks communicate by reading and writing to the same area of memory, which is protected by synchronization primitives like `Mutex` or `RwLock`. This is like a team of people all working on a single whiteboard. It's simple for basic cases, but can become chaotic and prone to bottlenecks as more people try to grab the same marker.
2. **Message-Passing Concurrency**: Tasks are completely isolated from one another. Each task owns its own data and state. They communicate by sending messages over a pre-

established communication channel. This is like a team communicating via memos or emails. It enforces a clear, structured flow of information.

Rust's philosophy, borrowed from languages like Erlang, can be summarized as: *"Do not communicate by sharing memory; instead, share memory by communicating."*

While Rust fully supports shared-state concurrency, its powerful channel implementations make message passing a clean, safe, and often preferred way to design complex applications.

What is a Channel?

A channel is a one-way pipe for sending data between asynchronous tasks. You create a channel and get back two halves: a **transmitter** (often called `tx` for short) and a **receiver** (`rx`).

- The `tx` half can be cloned and given to multiple tasks, allowing many "producers" to send data into the pipe.
- The `rx` half is unique and is held by the single "consumer" task that processes the data coming out of the pipe.

This setup is called an **MPSC channel**, which stands for **Multi-Producer, Single-Consumer**. It's the most common type of channel and is provided by Tokio in the `tokio::sync::mpsc` module.

Let's build a simple system where multiple worker tasks generate data and send it to a central processing task.

```
use tokio::sync::mpsc;
use tokio::time::{self, Duration};

// This task will generate some data.
async fn data_producer(id: u32, tx: mpsc::Sender<String>) {
    for i in 0..5 {
```

```rust
        let message = format!("Producer {} sending message #{}", id, i);
        println!("[{}] {}", tx.capacity(), message); // You can check channel capacity
        if tx.send(message).await.is_err() {
            // If send returns an error, it's because the receiver has been dropped.
            // The producer should probably stop its work.
            eprintln!("[Producer {}] Receiver dropped. Shutting down.", id);
            return;
        }
        time::sleep(Duration::from_millis(id as u64 * 100)).await;
    }
}

// This task will receive and process the data.
async fn data_consumer(mut rx: mpsc::Receiver<String>) {
    println!("[Consumer] Waiting for messages...");
    // `rx.recv()` returns `Some(message)` as long as there are active senders.
    // When all `tx` clones are dropped, `recv()` will return `None`, ending the loop.
    while let Some(message) = rx.recv().await {
        println!("[Consumer] GOT: {}", message);
    }
    println!("[Consumer] Channel closed. Shutting down.");
}

#[tokio::main]
async fn main() {
    // 1. Create a bounded channel with a capacity of 10.
    let (tx, rx) = mpsc::channel(10);

    // 2. Spawn the single consumer task.
    let consumer_handle = tokio::spawn(data_consumer(rx));
```

```rust
    // 3. Spawn multiple producer tasks.
    let mut producer_handles = vec![];
    for i in 1..=3 {
        // Clone the transmitter for each producer.
        let producer_tx = tx.clone();
        let handle = tokio::spawn(data_producer(i, producer_tx));
        producer_handles.push(handle);
    }

    // 4. Drop the original transmitter.
    // This is important! The receiver's loop will only end when ALL senders
    // (including the original `tx`) have been dropped.
    drop(tx);

    // Wait for all producers to finish their work.
    for handle in producer_handles {
        handle.await.unwrap();
    }

    // Finally, wait for the consumer to finish processing all messages.
    consumer_handle.await.unwrap();
}
```

Backpressure and Bounded Channels

When we created the channel with `mpsc::channel(10)`, we created a **bounded channel**. It has a fixed capacity and can only hold up to 10 messages in its internal buffer at a time. This is a critical feature for building resilient systems.

If the producers generate data faster than the consumer can process it, the channel will fill up. When a producer calls `tx.send(message).await` on a full channel, its task will be suspended until the consumer processes a message and makes space. This natural pausing is called **backpressure**. It prevents a slow consumer from being overwhelmed and prevents the channel from consuming an unbounded amount of memory.

For this reason, you should almost always use a bounded channel. While Tokio offers an `unbounded_channel`, it should be used with extreme caution, as a slow consumer could cause it to grow indefinitely, eventually crashing your application.

Other Types of Channels for Different Jobs

MPSC channels are the workhorse of async communication, but Tokio provides other specialized types:

- **oneshot**: A channel for sending a *single value*. It's perfect for when a task needs to send a one-time response back to a requester. The Actor Model often uses an MPSC channel for commands and a `oneshot` channel for replies.
- **broadcast**: A multi-producer, *multi-consumer* channel. When a value is sent, every active receiver gets a clone of it. This is ideal for "fan-out" events, like broadcasting a shutdown signal to all long-running tasks in an application.
- **watch**: A single-producer, multi-consumer channel for distributing state. It only ever holds one value—the most recent one. When a new value is sent, it overwrites the previous one. Receivers can check the current value at any time or wait for a change. This is great for distributing configuration updates.

Choosing the right channel for the job is a key part of your application's design. By using these message-passing primitives, you can build complex systems from simple, isolated tasks that communicate in a well-defined and safe manner, avoiding the complexities and potential deadlocks of shared-state concurrency.

Implementing the Actor Model for Better State Management

We've seen that `Arc<Mutex<T>>` is a valid way to share state, but as applications grow, it can lead to complexity. Spreading locks throughout your codebase can make the logic harder to follow and increases the risk of deadlocks, where two tasks are each waiting for a lock held by the other.

The **Actor Model** offers a more structured and often safer alternative. It's a design pattern that treats "actors" as the primitive units of computation. In our context, an actor is simply an asynchronous task that is solely responsible for a specific piece of state.

Here's how it works:

1. **State Encapsulation**: An actor owns its state completely. No other task can access it directly. For example, a `UserSessionActor` would own the `HashMap` of active user sessions.
2. **Message-Based Communication**: Other tasks can only interact with the actor by sending it messages over a channel. These messages are commands, like `AddUserSession` or `GetUserSession`.
3. **Serialized Processing**: The actor processes messages from its channel one at a time, in the order they are received. This is the key to its safety. Because it only does one thing at a time, there are no data races, and no locks are needed within the actor itself.

This model transforms scattered lock contention into a clean, sequential message queue, which is much easier to reason about.

Building Your First Actor

An actor in Tokio has a few standard components:

- A `struct` to hold the actor's state and its channel receiver.
- An `enum` to define the valid messages (commands) it can receive.
- An `async fn` (usually called `run` or `start`) that contains the actor's main loop for processing messages.

Let's refactor our shared counter example from the previous section to use the Actor Model instead of an `Arc<Mutex<T>>`.

```
use tokio::sync::mpsc;

// 1. Define the messages (commands) our actor can understand.

enum CounterCommand {

    Increment,

    // We'll add a way to get the value later.

}

// 2. Define the actor's struct. It owns the state and the channel receiver.

struct CounterActor {

    receiver: mpsc::Receiver<CounterCommand>,

    counter: i32,

}

impl CounterActor {

    // A simple constructor.

    fn new(receiver: mpsc::Receiver<CounterCommand>) -> Self
    {
```

```rust
    CounterActor {
        receiver,
        counter: 0,
    }
}

// 3. This is the actor's main loop where it processes messages.
async fn run(&mut self) {
    println!("[Actor] Started. Waiting for commands.");
    while let Some(command) = self.receiver.recv().await {
        match command {
            CounterCommand::Increment => {
                self.counter += 1;
                println!("[Actor] Counter is now: {}", self.counter);
            }
        }
    }
    println!("[Actor] Channel closed. Shutting down.");
}
}
```

```rust
#[tokio::main]
async fn main() {
    // Create the MPSC channel for sending commands to the actor.
    let (tx, rx) = mpsc::channel(32);
    // Create and run the actor.
    let mut actor = CounterActor::new(rx);
    // Spawn the actor's run loop as a background task.
    let actor_handle = tokio::spawn(async move {
        actor.run().await;
    });
    // Now, other tasks can send commands.
    // We'll send commands from the main task for this example.
    println!("[Main] Sending Increment commands...");
    for _ in 0..5 {
        // The send is async, but we don't need to wait for a reply here.
        tx.send(CounterCommand::Increment).await.unwrap();
    }
    // To see the actor shut down cleanly, we can drop the sender.
    drop(tx);
```

```rust
    // Wait for the actor to finish processing all messages.
    actor_handle.await.unwrap();
}
```

This code is clean and completely free of locks. All mutable access to the `counter` is centralized within the `run` method, which is guaranteed to execute sequentially.

Getting a Response from an Actor

The example above is great for "fire-and-forget" commands, but what if a task needs to ask the actor for a value? We can't send the `counter` value back on the main MPSC channel.

This is the perfect use case for a **tokio::sync::oneshot channel**. A `oneshot` channel, as its name implies, is used to send a single value one time. The requester can create a `oneshot` channel, package the `tx` half inside its command message, and `await` the `rx` half for the response.

Let's enhance our actor to handle requests for the current counter value.

```rust
use tokio::sync::{mpsc, oneshot};

// The new command includes a way to send a response back.
enum CounterCommand {
    Increment,
    GetValue {
        // The sender for the one-time response channel.
        responder: oneshot::Sender<i32>,
    },
```

```rust
}

struct CounterActor {
    receiver: mpsc::Receiver<CounterCommand>,
    counter: i32,
}

impl CounterActor {
    fn new(receiver: mpsc::Receiver<CounterCommand>) -> Self {
        CounterActor { receiver, counter: 0 }
    }

    async fn run(&mut self) {
        while let Some(command) = self.receiver.recv().await {
            match command {
                CounterCommand::Increment => {
                    self.counter += 1;
                }
                CounterCommand::GetValue { responder } => {
                    // The actor sends the current state back on the provided oneshot channel.
                    // We ignore the result of the send, as the requester might have
```

```rust
            // timed out and dropped the receiver.
            let _ = responder.send(self.counter);
            }
        }
      }
    }
}

#[tokio::main]
async fn main() {
    let (tx, rx) = mpsc::channel(32);
    let mut actor = CounterActor::new(rx);

    tokio::spawn(async move { actor.run().await });

    // Let's increment a few times.
    tx.send(CounterCommand::Increment).await.unwrap();
    tx.send(CounterCommand::Increment).await.unwrap();
    // Now, let's request the current value.
```

```rust
// 1. Create the oneshot channel for the response.

let (resp_tx, resp_rx) = oneshot::channel();

// 2. Send the command, including the sender half of our oneshot channel.

let cmd = CounterCommand::GetValue { responder: resp_tx };

tx.send(cmd).await.unwrap();

// 3. Await the response from the actor.

match resp_rx.await {

    Ok(value) => {

        println!("[Main] Received counter value: {}", value);

    }

    Err(_) => {

        eprintln!("[Main] The actor task shut down before it could respond.");

    }

}

// The final value should be 2.

assert_eq!(resp_rx.await.unwrap_or(-1), 2);

}
```

This request-response pattern is fundamental to the Actor Model. It keeps the state isolated and safe while allowing for complex, two-way interactions. By preferring this model, you can design sophisticated concurrent systems that are far less prone to the classic pitfalls of shared-state programming.

Managing Shared Application State with `Arc<Mutex<T>>`

We've just explored the Actor Model, a powerful pattern for isolating state and managing communication through messages. It's an excellent choice for complex components, promoting clean, decoupled code. However, it's not the only tool available, nor is it always the most direct solution.

Sometimes, the overhead of setting up an actor—with its command enums and message-passing loops—is more complex than necessary. For simpler or more localized state-sharing needs, falling back to the fundamental pattern of direct shared access using `Arc<Mutex<T>>` is often a more pragmatic and clearer choice. This section revisits this crucial pattern, exploring its trade-offs and the discipline required to use it safely and effectively in larger applications.

When is `Arc<Mutex<T>>` the Right Choice?

Choosing between the Actor Model and a shared `Mutex` is a key architectural decision. You might prefer `Arc<Mutex<T>>` when:

- **The State is Simple and Localized**: If you just need to share a simple counter, a boolean flag, or a small collection between a handful of closely related tasks, a `Mutex` is often simpler to set up and understand than a full-fledged actor.
- **Contention is Low**: If tasks only need to access the shared data infrequently, the cost of locking is minimal. The `Mutex` won't become a performance bottleneck because tasks rarely have to wait for each other.
- **Interactions are Brief**: The ideal use case is when a task needs to acquire a lock, perform a quick, synchronous

operation (like updating a value in a `HashMap`), and then immediately release the lock.

Let's look at a practical example: an application-wide cache for tracking the results of expensive computations. Multiple tasks might need to read from or write to this cache.

```rust
use std::collections::HashMap;

use std::sync::Arc;

use tokio::sync::Mutex;

use tokio::time::{self, Duration};

// A cache to store results of some "expensive" computation.

// The key is the input, the value is the result.

type ComputationCache = Arc<Mutex<HashMap<u32, String>>>;

// Simulates an expensive computation that we want to cache.

async fn expensive_computation(input: u32) -> String {

    println!("[COMPUTE] Performing expensive computation for input: {}", input);

    time::sleep(Duration::from_secs(1)).await;

    format!("Result-for-{}", input)

}

// A worker task that needs the result of a computation.

// It will first check the cache. If the result isn't there, it computes it,
```

```rust
// then stores it in the cache for other tasks to use.
async fn worker(id: u32, input: u32, cache: ComputationCache) {
    // Acquire a lock to check the cache.
    let mut locked_cache = cache.lock().await;
    if let Some(cached_result) = locked_cache.get(&input) {
        println!("[Worker {}] Found result in cache for input {}: '{}'", id, input, cached_result);
        // The lock is released automatically when `locked_cache` goes out of scope here.
        return;
    }
    // If we're here, the lock has been released. It's important to release the lock
    // before performing the long-running computation.
    drop(locked_cache);


    // Perform the computation while not holding the lock.
    let result = expensive_computation(input).await;
    // Now, acquire the lock again to store the new result.
    let mut locked_cache = cache.lock().await;
    locked_cache.insert(input, result.clone());
```

```rust
    println!("[Worker {}] Stored new result in cache for input {}", id, input);
}

#[tokio::main]
async fn main() {
    let cache: ComputationCache = Arc::new(Mutex::new(HashMap::new()));

    let mut handles = vec![];

    // Spawn several workers. Some will request the same computation.
    let inputs = [10, 20, 10, 30, 20, 20];

    for (i, &input) in inputs.iter().enumerate() {
        let cache_clone = Arc::clone(&cache);

        let handle = tokio::spawn(worker(i as u32, input, cache_clone));

        handles.push(handle);
    }

    for handle in handles {
        handle.await.unwrap();
    }

    println!("\nFinal cache state: {:?}", cache.lock().await);
```

}

The Cardinal Rule: Keep Your Locks Brief

The single most important principle when working with `Mutex` is to hold the lock for the shortest time possible. The period between when you acquire a lock and when you release it is a **critical section**. Nothing else that needs that lock can make progress. Notice the structure in the `worker` function above:

1. Lock the cache.
2. Perform a quick check (`.get()`).
3. **Immediately unlock the cache** (by dropping the lock guard `locked_cache`).
4. Perform the long-running operation (`expensive_computation`) **without holding the lock**.
5. Lock the cache again.
6. Perform another quick operation (`.insert()`).
7. The lock is released.

This is crucial. If we had held the lock during the one-second `sleep` inside `expensive_computation`, we would have frozen every other worker task for that entire second, completely defeating the purpose of concurrency.

An anti-pattern to avoid:

```
// WRONG: Don't do this!

async fn wrong_worker(cache: ComputationCache) {

    let mut locked_cache = cache.lock().await;

    // We are holding the lock while we .await another future!

    // This blocks all other tasks from accessing the cache for the entire duration.

    let result = expensive_computation(42).await; // <-- BAD
```

```
        locked_cache.insert(42, result);
}
```

Holding locks across `.await` points is one of the most common and severe bugs in async Rust. It serializes your execution and can easily lead to deadlocks if the awaited future also needs to acquire locks. The rule is simple: get in, do your synchronous work, and get out.

The Danger of Deadlocks

A deadlock occurs when two or more tasks are stuck waiting for each other to release a resource. With mutexes, the classic scenario is:

- Task A locks `Mutex 1`.
- Task B locks `Mutex 2`.
- Task A now tries to lock `Mutex 2` and waits because Task B holds it.
- Task B now tries to lock `Mutex 1` and waits because Task A holds it.

Both tasks are now frozen forever. Neither can proceed. While the Actor Model can help avoid this by centralizing state, you can also prevent it when using mutexes by following a simple rule: **if you need to acquire multiple locks, always acquire them in the same, fixed order everywhere in your codebase.** This prevents the circular dependency that creates the deadlock.

Ultimately, `Arc<Mutex<T>>` is a lower-level, more fundamental primitive than an actor. It gives you direct control but demands more discipline. For many common patterns, its simplicity is an advantage, as long as you remain vigilant about keeping your critical sections short and avoiding deadlocks.

Chapter 4:
Advanced Async Techniques and Patterns

Now that we have a solid foundation in structuring concurrent applications, it's time to explore some of the more advanced, powerful features in the async ecosystem. This chapter will equip you with the tools to solve more complex problems, from handling continuous flows of data to gracefully integrating blocking code and building custom `Future`s.

We'll start with a concept that is fundamental to handling data-intensive applications: the `Stream`.

Processing Continuous Data with the `Stream` Trait

So far, we've dealt with `Future`s that resolve to a single value. You `.await` the future, and eventually, you get one result back. But what about situations where you have a sequence of values arriving over time?

- Messages arriving from a websocket connection.
- Rows being returned from a large database query.
- Events from a message queue like RabbitMQ or Kafka.
- Notifications from the file system about changed files.

These are not single events; they are **streams** of data. A `Stream` in async Rust is the equivalent of the standard library's `Iterator`. While an iterator produces a sequence of values synchronously with a `next()` method, a stream produces a sequence of values asynchronously. You don't just call `next()`; you `.await` the next item.

The `Stream` trait (provided by the `futures` crate, which is a core dependency of Tokio) has one primary method:
```
fn poll_next(self: Pin<&mut Self>, cx: &mut Context<'_>) -> Poll<Option<Self::Item>>;
```

This looks very similar to a `Future`'s `poll` method. When polled, a stream can return:

- `Poll::Ready(Some(item))`: The next item in the stream is ready.
- `Poll::Ready(None)`: The stream has finished and will produce no more items.
- `Poll::Pending`: The stream is not finished, but the next item isn't ready yet (e.g., waiting for more data on the network).

Consuming a Stream

The `tokio-stream` crate provides utilities for working with streams, including a convenient `StreamExt` trait that adds many useful methods, much like `Iterator`'s extension methods.

The most common way to consume a stream is with a `while let` loop.

Let's look at a simple example. We'll create a stream that yields a number every second. First, add `tokio-stream` to your `Cargo.toml`:

```toml
[dependencies]

tokio = { version = "1", features = ["full"] }

tokio-stream = "0.1"
```

Now, the code:

```rust
use tokio_stream::StreamExt;
use tokio::time::{self, Duration};

#[tokio::main]
async fn main() {
    // We create a stream from a simple interval timer.
    // This stream will produce an item every 1 second.
```

```rust
    let mut stream = tokio_stream::iter(1..=5)
        .throttle(Duration::from_secs(1));

    println!("Starting to consume the stream...");

    // The `while let Some(value)` loop is the idiomatic way to process a stream.
    // The loop will automatically end when the stream returns `None`.
    while let Some(value) = stream.next().await {
        println!("Received from stream: {}", value);
    }

    println!("Stream has finished.");
}
```

The `.next().await` call inside the loop will pause execution until the stream either yields its next item or finishes. This is an incredibly powerful and clean way to write logic that responds to a sequence of events.

Transforming Streams with Combinators

Just like iterators, streams have a rich set of **combinator** methods that allow you to chain operations to transform, filter, and manipulate the data. `StreamExt` provides familiar methods like `map` and `filter`.

Let's enhance our previous example to only process even numbers and to square them before printing.

```rust
use tokio_stream::StreamExt;

#[tokio::main]
async fn main() {

    println!("Consuming a transformed stream...");
```

```rust
// Start with a stream of numbers from 1 to 10.
let mut stream = tokio_stream::iter(1..=10)
    .filter(|&x| {
        // This is an async filter. We return a future that resolves to a boolean.
        // For this simple case, we can use an `async` block.
        async move {
            println!("[Filter] Checking {}", x);
            x % 2 == 0
        }
    })
    .map(|x| {
        // This map operation is synchronous, but it could also be async.
        println!("[Map] Mapping {}", x);
        x * x
    });

while let Some(value) = stream.next().await {
    println!("Processed value: {}", value);
}
```

}

This functional-style chaining is very expressive. Each item from the original stream flows through the `filter` and then the `map` before being consumed by our `while` loop.

Backpressure Revisited

Streams are a natural fit for handling **backpressure**. In the example above, if the processing inside the `while` loop was slow, the stream would simply wait. The `filter` and `map` operations would only be called when the main loop was ready for the next item by calling `.next().await`. This prevents an overwhelming flood of data. When you design a system where one component produces data (a stream) and another consumes it, this backpressure mechanism happens naturally, leading to more stable and resilient applications.

Understanding streams is essential for building data-driven applications in async Rust. They provide a clean, composable, and efficient abstraction for handling any kind of sequential data that arrives over time.

When and Why to Write Your Own `Future`: A Look at `Pin<T>`

Up to this point, we have been consumers of `Future`s. We get them from `async fn` calls or from library functions like `tokio::time::sleep`, and we use `.await` to run them. For most application development, this is all you will ever need.

However, to truly master asynchronous Rust, it's valuable to understand what a `Future` is under the hood. Knowing how to build one from scratch unlocks the ability to create highly optimized, specialized async logic or to wrap non-async, callback-based APIs into the `async/await` world.

Before we can build a `Future`, we must first understand one of the most mysterious yet fundamental concepts in async Rust: `Pin<T>`.

The Core Problem: Why `Pin` Exists

When the Rust compiler transforms an `async` block into a `Future`, it creates a special kind of `struct`. This struct needs to hold all the state of the function across `.await` points. This includes all local variables.

Consider this `async` block:

```rust
async {
    let my_data = [0; 128]; // Some data on the stack

    let reference_to_data = &my_data[0]; // A reference to that data

    some_other_future().await; // <- We pause here

    println!("The first byte is: {}", reference_to_data);
}
```

The compiled `Future` struct for this block would look something like this, conceptually:

```rust
struct MyFuture {
    state: i32, // To track if we're before or after the .await

    my_data: [u8; 128],

    // This reference points to a field *within the same struct*.
    reference_to_data: *const u8, // Using a raw pointer for the example
}
```

This is a **self-referential struct**. One of its fields (`reference_to_data`) contains a pointer to another field (`my_data`) within the same struct.

In normal Rust, this is a huge problem. Rust values can be moved in memory at any time (for example, when passing them into a function or returning them). If we moved `MyFuture` to a new memory location, the `my_data` field would move with it, but the `reference_to_data` pointer would still be pointing to the *old* memory location. It would now be a dangling pointer, leading to undefined behavior.

This is where `Pin` comes in. A `Pin<T>` is a special kind of pointer that guarantees that the value it points to, the `T`, will never be moved in memory again for the rest of its lifetime. It "pins" the data to its location. By wrapping our self-referential `Future` in a `Pin`, the async executor can safely poll it, knowing that its internal pointers will always remain valid.

You will rarely interact with `Pin` directly unless you are writing low-level async code, but every time you `.await`, the compiler and runtime are using `Pin` to guarantee safety.

Building a Custom Future: A Simple Timer
Now that we understand the "why" of `Pin`, let's build our own simple `Future` that completes after a specified duration. This will show us how a `Future` communicates its state (`Pending` or `Ready`) back to the executor.

We will need to implement the `std::future::Future` trait, which has a single method, `poll`.

```rust
use std::future::Future;

use std::pin::Pin;
```

```rust
use std::task::{Context, Poll};

use std::time::{Duration, Instant};

use std::thread;

// Our custom Future struct.

pub struct SimpleTimer {

    deadline: Instant,

}

impl SimpleTimer {

    // A constructor to create a new timer.

    pub fn new(duration: Duration) -> Self {

        SimpleTimer {

            deadline: Instant::now() + duration,

        }

    }

}

// Implement the Future trait for our SimpleTimer.

impl Future for SimpleTimer {

    type Output = String; // The type of value this future will produce.

    // The poll method is the heart of the Future.
```

```rust
fn poll(self: Pin<&mut Self>, cx: &mut Context<'_>) -> Poll<Self::Output> {

    let now = Instant::now();

    if self.deadline <= now {

        // The deadline has passed. The future is complete.

        // We return Poll::Ready with our output value.

        println!("[Timer] Deadline reached. Future is complete.");

        Poll::Ready("Timer finished!".to_string())

    } else {

        // The deadline has not been reached yet. The future is not complete.

        // We need to tell the executor to poll us again later.

        println!("[Timer] Not yet complete. Will wake up later.");

        // Get a handle to the Waker from the context.

        let waker = cx.waker().clone();

        let deadline = self.deadline;

        // Spawn a new thread to "wake up" the task when the time is right.

        // This is a simplified approach for demonstration. A real runtime's

        // timer is far more efficient.
```

```rust
        thread::spawn(move || {

            let now = Instant::now();

            if now < deadline {

                thread::sleep(deadline - now);

            }

            // Once the time has passed, we call `wake()`. This tells the executor
            // that our task is ready to be polled again.

            println!("[Waker Thread] Time is up! Waking the task.");

            waker.wake();

        });

        // Return Poll::Pending to indicate that the future is not yet finished.

        Poll::Pending

    }

}

}

// We can now use our custom future in an async block.

#[tokio::main]

async fn main() {
```

```rust
    println!("[Main] Starting a custom timer future for 2 seconds.");

    let timer = SimpleTimer::new(Duration::from_secs(2));

    // .await will drive our future's poll method.
    let result = timer.await;

    println!("[Main] The custom future completed with result: '{}'", result);
}
```

Let's break down the `poll` method:
1. **The `Pin<&mut Self>`**: The `poll` method receives the future wrapped in a `Pin`. This is the safety guarantee that allows us to work with it.
2. **The `Context` and `Waker`**: The `Context` (cx) is how the `Future` communicates with the async runtime. The most important thing inside the context is the `Waker`. The `Waker` is a handle that, when its `wake()` method is called, notifies the executor that the task associated with it is ready to be polled again.
3. **The `Poll` Enum**: Our method must return either `Poll::Ready(value)` if it's finished, or `Poll::Pending` if it's not.
4. **The Logic**: If our timer's deadline has passed, we return `Ready`. If not, we do something crucial: we clone the `waker` and send it to another thread. That thread waits until the deadline and then calls `waker.wake()`. This `wake()` call is the signal that tells the executor, "Hey, it's time to try polling that timer task again." On the next poll, the deadline will have passed, and the future will finally return `Ready`.

While you may not write custom Futures every day, understanding this poll -> Pending -> wake() -> poll -> Ready cycle is the key to understanding the inner workings of async/await in Rust. It demystifies the magic and shows you the safe, low-level machinery that makes high-performance concurrency possible.

Integrating Blocking, Synchronous Code Without Freezing the Runtime

The asynchronous world is ideal, but it's not the entire world. You will inevitably need to use a library or perform a calculation that was not designed for async/await. These pieces of synchronous code often have one dangerous characteristic: they block.

- A database driver that doesn't have an async API will block the thread during network I/O.
- A CPU-intensive task, like hashing a password, resizing an image, or compressing a file, will monopolize a CPU core, preventing it from doing other work.
- An older library that makes synchronous HTTP requests will block while waiting for the remote server.

If you call one of these blocking functions directly from within an async task, you commit the cardinal sin of async programming: **blocking the executor**. A Tokio worker thread is responsible for juggling hundreds or thousands of tasks. When you block it, you freeze all of them. The scheduler grinds to a halt, latency skyrockets, and the benefits of asynchrony evaporate.

So, how do we safely bridge the synchronous and asynchronous worlds? Tokio provides an essential escape hatch: tokio::task::spawn_blocking.

The Solution: A Dedicated Thread Pool

The `spawn_blocking` function is your safe gateway to the blocking world. It works by maintaining a separate, dedicated thread pool specifically for running blocking code.

When you give a blocking function to `spawn_blocking`:

1. Tokio takes your function and moves it over to one of the threads in this special blocking pool.
2. Your original async task that called `spawn_blocking` is suspended, just as if it were awaiting any other `Future`. The worker thread it was on is now free to run other async tasks.
3. The blocking function runs to completion on its dedicated thread. Because this thread is not part of the main async worker pool, it's perfectly safe for it to be blocked.
4. Once the blocking function is finished, it signals the Tokio runtime. The runtime then wakes up your original async task, which can now receive the result and continue.

This strategy effectively quarantines the blocking behavior, protecting the performance and responsiveness of your main async scheduler.

A Practical Example: Password Hashing

Let's look at a very common and realistic scenario: hashing a user's password during registration in a web application. Password hashing algorithms like `bcrypt` or `argon2` are designed to be computationally expensive to make brute-force attacks difficult. This means they are CPU-bound and will block a thread.

First, add the `bcrypt` crate to your `Cargo.toml`:

```
[dependencies]

tokio = { version = "1", features = ["full"] }
```

bcrypt = "0.15"

Now, let's see the right way and the wrong way to do this.

```rust
use tokio::task;

use std::time::Instant;

// This is a synchronous, CPU-intensive function.
// It will block whatever thread it runs on.
fn hash_password_sync(password: String) -> Result<String, bcrypt::BcryptError> {
    println!("[HASH_SYNC] Starting password hash calculation...");
    let start = Instant::now();
    let result = bcrypt::hash(password, 12); // `12` is the cost factor
    println!("[HASH_SYNC] Finished hashing. Elapsed: {:?}", start.elapsed());
    result
}

// The WRONG way to call a blocking function.
async fn block_the_runtime_badly() {
    println!("\n--- Running the BAD example: Calling blocking code directly ---");
    let start = Instant::now();
    // This will freeze the worker thread, hurting the performance of all other tasks.
```

```rust
    let _ = hash_password_sync("my-super-secret-password-1".to_string());
    println!("--- BAD example finished. Total time: {:?} ---", start.elapsed());
}
// The RIGHT way to call a blocking function.
async fn run_blocking_code_correctly() {
    println!("\n--- Running the GOOD example: Using spawn_blocking ---");
    let start = Instant::now();
    let password = "my-super-secret-password-2".to_string();
    // `spawn_blocking` moves the blocking function to a dedicated thread pool.
    // The `.await` here waits for the result without blocking the current worker thread.
    let hash_result = task::spawn_blocking(move || {
        hash_password_sync(password)
    }).await;
    // The outer `Result` is from the JoinHandle (in case of a panic).
    // The inner `Result` is from our `bcrypt::hash` function.
    match hash_result {
        Ok(Ok(hash)) => {
```

```rust
            println!("Password hashed successfully: {:.20}...", hash);
        }
        Ok(Err(e)) => {
            eprintln!("Bcrypt error: {}", e);
        }
        Err(e) => {
            eprintln!("Spawn_blocking task panicked: {}", e);
        }
    }
    println!("--- GOOD example finished. Total time: {:?} ---", start.elapsed());
}
#[tokio::main]
async fn main() {
    // To demonstrate the impact, we'll run another async task concurrently.
    tokio::spawn(async {
        let mut i = 0;
        loop {
            tokio::time::sleep(tokio::time::Duration::from_millis(100)).await;
            println!("[Background Task] Alive... {}", i);
```

```
            i += 1;
        }
    });
    block_the_runtime_badly().await;
    run_blocking_code_correctly().await;
}
```

If you run this code, you will notice a stark difference in the output. During `block_the_runtime_badly`, the "[Background Task]" will stop printing completely. The entire executor is frozen. In contrast, during `run_blocking_code_correctly`, the background task continues to print its "Alive..." messages without interruption, because the expensive hashing work has been successfully offloaded.

`spawn_blocking` is an indispensable tool for pragmatism. It acknowledges that not all code is asynchronous and provides a safe, efficient bridge to the synchronous world, ensuring your application remains responsive and performant.

While `abort()` has its uses, it should be treated with caution. It is not cooperative. The task gets no warning and has no chance to perform cleanup. It's like pulling the plug on a computer instead of using the shutdown menu.

For building resilient, predictable systems, the graceful shutdown pattern using signals and `select!` is almost always the superior approach. It makes your application's lifecycle explicit and ensures that when it's time to stop, it does so with precision and safety.

Cancellation and Graceful Shutdown

A concurrent application is like a symphony orchestra. You can't just have the musicians stop playing whenever they feel like it; the piece would fall apart. Likewise, you can't just abruptly kill your application's process. Doing so could leave files half-written, database transactions incomplete, and user data in a corrupted state.

A robust application must be able to shut down cleanly. This process, known as **graceful shutdown**, is a critical feature that you must design into your system from the very beginning. It involves signaling all running tasks that it's time to stop, giving them a chance to finish their current work, clean up their resources, and exit in an orderly fashion.

The Core Pattern: The Shutdown Signal

The most common and effective way to implement graceful shutdown is with a "shutdown signal." This is typically a tokio::sync::broadcast channel.

Why a broadcast channel? Because it allows one sender to notify *many* receivers. Your main application logic can hold the single Sender, and every long-running task you spawn can be given a Receiver. When it's time to shut down, you send a single message on the channel, and every task gets notified simultaneously.

But how does a task listen for a shutdown signal *while also doing its normal work*? The answer lies in one of Tokio's most powerful macros: tokio::select!.

The select! macro allows a task to wait on multiple different asynchronous operations at the same time. It will execute the code block corresponding to the *first* operation that completes, and cancel the others. This is perfect for our use case: we want a task to either do its work *or* react to a shutdown signal, whichever comes first.

A Practical Implementation

Let's build a small application with several background workers. We will use a broadcast channel to signal them to shut down, and we'll even listen for the Ctrl+C keyboard command to trigger the shutdown, just like a real server would.

```rust
use tokio::sync::broadcast;
use tokio::time::{self, Duration};

// This function represents a long-running worker task.
async fn worker_task(id: u32, mut shutdown_receiver: broadcast::Receiver<()>) {
    println!("[Worker {}] Started.", id);
    let mut i = 0;
    loop {
        // The `select!` macro waits on multiple branches.
        tokio::select! {
            // Branch 1: The task's actual work.
            // In this case, we just sleep for a second.
            _ = time::sleep(Duration::from_secs(1)) => {
                i += 1;
                println!("[Worker {}] Still working... (cycle {})", id, i);
            }

            // Branch 2: The shutdown signal.
            // This branch completes if a message is received on the shutdown channel.
            _ = shutdown_receiver.recv() => {
                println!("[Worker {}] Shutdown signal received! Cleaning up and exiting.", id);
                // Here you would perform any necessary cleanup, like saving state to disk.
                break; // Exit the loop.
            }
        }
    }
}
```

```rust
    println!("[Worker {}] Exited.", id);
}

#[tokio::main]
async fn main() {
    // 1. Create the broadcast channel for the shutdown signal.
    // The channel's capacity doesn't matter much here since we send a single value.
    let (shutdown_tx, _) = broadcast::channel(1);
    let mut handles = vec![];

    println!("[Main] Spawning 3 worker tasks.");
    for i in 1..=3 {
        // 2. Create a new receiver for each worker.
        let shutdown_rx = shutdown_tx.subscribe();
        // 3. Spawn the worker, giving it its receiver.
        let handle = tokio::spawn(worker_task(i, shutdown_rx));
        handles.push(handle);
    }

    // 4. Set up a listener for the Ctrl+C signal.
    // `tokio::signal::ctrl_c()` returns a future that completes when the signal is received.
    println!("[Main] Application running. Press Ctrl+C to shut down gracefully.");
    tokio::select! {
        _ = tokio::signal::ctrl_c() => {
            println!("\n[Main] Ctrl+C received. Sending shutdown signal...");
        }
        _ = time::sleep(Duration::from_secs(10)) => {
            // As a fallback, we'll also shut down after 10 seconds.
            println!("\n[Main] 10 seconds elapsed. Sending shutdown signal...");
        }
    }
```

```rust
    // 5. Send the shutdown signal.
    // We ignore the result, as there might be no active receivers if tasks ended early.
    let _ = shutdown_tx.send(());

    println!("[Main] Waiting for all worker tasks to exit...");
    for handle in handles {
        handle.await.unwrap();
    }

    println!("[Main] All tasks have shut down. Exiting.");
}
```

When you run this program, the workers will happily print their "Still working..." messages. When you press `Ctrl+C`, you will see them all receive the signal and exit their loops cleanly. This is the essence of cooperative, graceful shutdown.

Task Cancellation: The Abrupt Alternative

There is another way to stop a task: by force. Every `JoinHandle` has an `abort()` method. Calling `handle.abort()` immediately terminates the target task. The `.await` on its `JoinHandle` will then return an `Err` with a `JoinError` indicating it was cancelled.

While `abort()` has its uses, it should be treated with extreme caution. It is not cooperative; it's **preemptive**. The task gets no warning and has no chance to perform cleanup. It's like pulling the plug on a computer instead of using the shutdown menu. When you `abort` a task, it stops at the next `.await` point it hits, regardless of what it was in the middle of doing.

This can leave your application in an inconsistent state. Consider a task that performs a multi-step operation:

```rust
use tokio::fs::{self, File};
```

```rust
use tokio::io::AsyncWriteExt;
use tokio::time::{self, Duration};

// A task that creates a temporary file, writes to it, and should clean it up.
async fn file_worker() {
    let tmp_file_path = "temp_data.tmp";
    println!("[File Worker] Creating temporary file: {}", tmp_file_path);
    let mut file = File::create(tmp_file_path).await.unwrap();

    // Imagine a long-running operation here.
    println!("[File Worker] Performing work...");
    file.write_all(b"important intermediate data").await.unwrap();

    // This task will be aborted while it's sleeping here.
    time::sleep(Duration::from_secs(10)).await;

    // This cleanup code will NEVER be reached if the task is aborted.
    println!("[File Worker] Work complete. Deleting temporary file.");
    fs::remove_file(tmp_file_path).await.unwrap();
}

#[tokio::main]
async fn main() {
    let handle = tokio::spawn(file_worker());

    // Give the worker a moment to create the file.
    time::sleep(Duration::from_secs(1)).await;

    println!("[Main] Aborting the file worker task forcefully...");
    handle.abort();

    let res = handle.await;
```

```rust
        println!("[Main] Worker task join result: {:?}", res);
        if res.is_err() && res.unwrap_err().is_cancelled() {
            println!("[Main] The task was successfully cancelled.");
        }

        // Check if the temporary file was left behind.
        match fs::metadata("temp_data.tmp").await {
            Ok(_) => println!("[Main] DANGER: Temporary file was not cleaned up!"),
            Err(_) => println!("[Main] Temporary file was successfully cleaned up."),
        }

        // Clean up manually for the example run.
        let _ = fs::remove_file("temp_data.tmp").await;
}
```

In this example, the file_worker is aborted while it's "working". Because the abortion is immediate, the task never reaches the fs::remove_file line. The temporary file is leaked, left behind on the disk. The same principle applies to other resources: a Mutex lock guard might not be dropped (poisoning the mutex), a database transaction could be left open, or a network connection might not be closed cleanly.

An operation is only "cancellation-safe" if it can be aborted at any .await point without violating invariants or leaking resources. Writing cancellation-safe code is difficult and requires careful design. For building resilient, predictable systems, the graceful shutdown pattern using signals and select! is almost always the superior approach. It makes your application's lifecycle explicit and ensures that when it's time to stop, it does so with precision and safety. Reserve abort() for situations where a task is completely unresponsive and you have no other choice but to terminate it forcefully, fully aware of the potential risks.

Chapter 5:
Building a Real-World Application: A Concurrent Web Service

Welcome to the most hands-on chapter of the book. All the theory and individual components we've learned—`async/await`, `tokio::spawn`, channels, mutexes, graceful shutdown—are about to come together. Over the course of this chapter, we will build a complete, high-performance, in-memory key-value store accessible via a web API.

This project will allow us to see how these concepts work together in a real-world scenario. By the end, you'll have a functioning web service that you can test, benchmark, and extend.

Project Overview: A High-Performance Key-Value Store

Our goal is to build a service with a simple HTTP API that allows clients to perform basic CRUD (Create, Read, Update, Delete) operations on string-based keys and values. The API will look like this:

- `GET /keys/:key`: Retrieve the value for a given key.
- `POST /keys`: Set a new key-value pair.
- `DELETE /keys/:key`: Delete a key-value pair.

We will use the best tools from the async ecosystem to build it:

- **Tokio**: As our core asynchronous runtime.
- **Axum**: A modern, ergonomic, and highly performant web framework built by the Tokio team.
- **Serde**: For serializing and deserializing JSON data.
- **DashMap**: A blazingly fast, concurrent `HashMap` for our in-memory storage.

Let's begin by setting up the web server.

Setting Up the Server and Handling Requests with Axum

Axum is a web application framework that leverages the power of Tokio and a library of middleware components called Tower. Its design philosophy is to be simple, predictable, and highly modular, making it an excellent choice for building robust services.

1. Project Setup

First, let's set up a new binary project (`cargo new kv-store`) and add our initial dependencies to `Cargo.toml`:

```toml
[dependencies]

tokio = { version = "1", features = ["full"] }

axum = "0.7"

serde = { version = "1.0", features = ["derive"] }
```

The Core Concepts: Handlers and Routers

An Axum application is built around two core concepts:
- **Handlers**: These are asynchronous functions that take a request as input and return a response. Each handler is responsible for the logic of a specific API endpoint.
- **Router**: The router is responsible for mapping incoming request paths (like `/` or `/users/123`) to the correct handler function.

Let's create our first, very simple handler. In `src/main.rs`, we can write a function that will handle requests to the root of our web server (`/`).

```rust
use axum::{

    routing::get,

    Router,
```

};

// This is our first request handler.

// It's a simple async function that returns a string slice.

// Axum knows how to convert common types like `&'static str` into an HTTP response.

async fn root_handler() -> &'static str {

  "Hello, World from our Axum server!"

}

Building the Application and Starting the Server

Now that we have a handler, we need to create a `Router`, tell it about our handler, and start a server to listen for requests.

We do this in our `main` function, which will be marked with `#[tokio::main]` as we've learned.

```
use axum::{

    routing::get,

    Router,

};

use tokio::net::TcpListener;

use std::net::SocketAddr;

async fn root_handler() -> &'static str {

    "Hello, World from our Axum server!"

}
```

```rust
#[tokio::main]
async fn main() {
    // 1. Define the application's routes.
    // We create a new router and tell it that GET requests to the "/" path
    // should be handled by our `root_handler` function.
    let app = Router::new().route("/", get(root_handler));

    // 2. Define the address to listen on.
    let addr = SocketAddr::from(([127, 0, 0, 1], 3000));

    println!("Server listening on http://{}", addr);

    // 3. Create a TCP listener and bind it to the address.
    let listener = TcpListener::bind(addr).await.unwrap();

    // 4. Serve the application.
    // `axum::serve` takes the listener and our router, and starts handling
    // incoming HTTP requests. This will run forever until the process is killed.
    axum::serve(listener, app).await.unwrap();
}
```

This is a complete, functioning web server. Let's break it down:

1. **`Router::new().route("/", get(root_handler))`**: We create a new `Router`. The

`.route()` method takes a path (`/`) and a "service." `get(root_handler)` is a function provided by Axum that creates a service that only responds to `GET` requests and forwards them to `root_handler`.
2. **TcpListener::bind(addr).await**: We use Tokio's asynchronous `TcpListener` to create a socket that will listen for incoming connections on `127.0.0.1:3000`.
3. **axum::serve(listener, app).await**: This is the magic line. We hand our listener and our router to Axum's `serve` function. This function contains the main server loop that accepts new connections and passes them to our router to be handled. It's an async function that runs forever, so we `.await` it.

You can now run your application with `cargo run`. You will see the "Server listening..." message. If you open a web browser and navigate to `http://127.0.0.1:3000`, you will see the message "Hello, World from our Axum server!"

We have successfully set up the skeleton of our web service. In the next sections, we will build on this foundation by adding routes for our key-value store, handling JSON data, and managing our application's shared state.

Implementing the Core Logic with Concurrent Data Structures

Now that we have a running Axum server, it's time to implement the heart of our application: the key-value store itself. We need a place to store our data in memory, and this data needs to be safely accessible by the many concurrent tasks that Axum will spawn to handle incoming requests.

The Challenge: Choosing the Right Tool for Shared State

Our first instinct might be to use the tools we're already familiar with: a standard `std::collections::HashMap` wrapped in a `tokio::sync::Mutex` and an `Arc`. The pattern `Arc<Mutex<HashMap<String, String>>>` would certainly work, and it would be safe.

However, let's think about the performance implications in a web server context. A `Mutex` provides *exclusive* access. If one request handler acquires a lock on the `HashMap` to write a value, every other request—even those that just want to read a different value—must wait. On a server handling hundreds of requests per second, this single lock can become a major performance bottleneck, serializing access and neutralizing the benefits of our concurrent web server.

For a read-heavy or write-heavy workload on a shared collection, we can do better. We need a data structure designed from the ground up for high concurrency.

A Better Solution: DashMap

This is where the `dashmap` crate comes in. `DashMap` is a concurrent `HashMap`. Instead of using one single lock to protect the entire map, it uses a clever technique where the map is broken up into many smaller, independent shards, each with its own lock.

When you access a key, `DashMap` hashes the key to determine which shard it belongs to and only locks that specific shard. This means that two different tasks trying to access two different keys (that hash to different shards) can do so in parallel, without blocking each other. This dramatically reduces lock contention and significantly improves performance in highly concurrent scenarios like a web server.

1. Adding Dependencies
Let's add `dashmap` and a few other necessary crates to our `Cargo.toml`. We'll also add `serde_json` for working with JSON data.

```toml
[dependencies]
tokio = { version = "1", features = ["full"] }
axum = "0.7"
serde = { version = "1.0", features = ["derive"] }
serde_json = "1.0"
dashmap = "5.5"
```

Defining and Sharing Application State

The standard way to share state across handlers in Axum is to define a state `struct` or `type` and pass it to the `Router`. We'll create a type alias for our store to make the code cleaner.

In `src/main.rs`, let's define our state and update our `main` function to create and share it.

```rust
use axum::{
    routing::{get, post}, // We'll need post soon
    Router,
};
use dashmap::DashMap;
use std::sync::Arc;
use std::net::SocketAddr;
use tokio::net::TcpListener;

// Define a type alias for our shared state.
// Arc is used for safe, shared ownership across threads.
type AppState = Arc<DashMap<String, String>>;

#[tokio::main]
async fn main() {
    // Create the shared state (our key-value store).
    let shared_state = AppState::new(DashMap::new());

    // Build the router and add the state.
```

```rust
    // .with_state() makes the `shared_state` available to all handlers.
    let app = Router::new()
        .route("/", get(root_handler))
        // We'll add our new routes here soon
        .with_state(shared_state);

    let addr = SocketAddr::from(([127, 0, 0, 1], 3000));
    println!("Server listening on http://{}", addr);
    let listener = TcpListener::bind(addr).await.unwrap();
    axum::serve(listener, app).await.unwrap();
}

async fn root_handler() -> &'static str {
    "Hello, World from our key-value store!"
}
```

By using `.with_state(shared_state)`, we've instructed Axum that any handler on this router can now accept our `AppState` as an argument. Axum will handle the dependency injection for us.

3. Implementing the API Handlers

Now we can write the handlers for our API. Each handler will take the application state as an argument, along with any other needed extractors.

- **Extractors** are types that tell Axum how to pull data from an incoming request. `Path(T)` extracts from the URL path, and `Json(T)` deserializes the request body as JSON.

Let's implement the `GET /keys/:key` handler first.

```rust
use axum::{
    extract::{Path, State},
    http::StatusCode,
    response::IntoResponse,
    Json,
};
```

```rust
use serde::Deserialize;

// GET /keys/:key
// This handler retrieves a value for a given key.
async fn get_key(
    State(state): State<AppState>,
    Path(key): Path<String>,
) -> impl IntoResponse {
    // Try to get the value from the DashMap.
    if let Some(value_ref) = state.get(&key) {
        // The value from DashMap is a reference, so we clone it to return.
        let value = value_ref.clone();
        (StatusCode::OK, Json(value))
    } else {
        // If the key doesn't exist, return a 404 Not Found.
        (StatusCode::NOT_FOUND, Json("Key not found".to_string()))
    }
}
```

Next, let's implement the `POST /keys` handler. This will require a struct to represent the incoming JSON payload.

```rust
// A struct for the POST request body.
// `Deserialize` allows it to be created from JSON.
#[derive(Deserialize)]
struct CreatePayload {
    key: String,
    value: String,
}

// POST /keys
// This handler sets a new key-value pair.
async fn create_key(
    State(state): State<AppState>,
    Json(payload): Json<CreatePayload>,
```

```
) -> impl IntoResponse {
    // Insert the key-value pair into the DashMap.
    state.insert(payload.key, payload.value);
    StatusCode::CREATED // Return a 201 Created status.
}
```

Finally, we need to add these new handlers to our `Router` in the `main` function.

```
// Inside main()
let app = Router::new()
    .route("/", get(root_handler))
    .route("/keys", post(create_key)) // Add the POST route
    .route("/keys/:key", get(get_key))  // Add the GET route
    .with_state(shared_state);
```

Our server now has a functioning, concurrent in-memory store. The `DashMap` handles all the locking internally, so our handler logic remains clean and simple. We don't have to write `.lock().await` anywhere; we can just interact with the map directly, and `dashmap` ensures that all operations are thread-safe and highly parallelizable.

Adding Layers: Middleware for Logging and Authentication

Our key-value store is now functional, but real-world services require more than just core business logic. We need to handle **cross-cutting concerns**—features that apply across many different parts of the application, such as logging every incoming request, checking if a user is authenticated, handling compression, or adding security headers.

Manually adding this logic to every single handler function would be incredibly repetitive and error-prone. This is the problem that **middleware** solves.

What is Middleware?

You can think of middleware as a series of processing layers that a request must pass through on its way to your handler, and that the response passes through on its way back to the client. Each layer can inspect or modify the request/response, or even decide to stop the processing altogether (e.g., by returning an error).

```
Request -> Middleware 1 (Logging) -> Middleware 2 (Auth) -> Your Handler Response <- Middleware 1 (Logging) <- Middleware 2 (Auth) <- Your Handler
```

Axum's middleware system is built on top of a powerful library called `tower`. This gives us access to a rich ecosystem of ready-made middleware and makes it straightforward to write our own.

Using Pre-built Middleware: Request Logging

One of the first things you'll want for any web service is visibility into the requests it's receiving. The `tower-http` crate provides a `TraceLayer` that can automatically log details about every request and response.

1. Add Dependencies

Let's add `tower-http` and the `tracing` ecosystem crates to our `Cargo.toml`. `tracing` is the standard library for instrumenting Rust applications.

[dependencies] [dependencies]

tokio = { version = "1", features = ["full"] }

axum = "0.7"

serde = { version = "1.0", features = ["derive"] }

serde_json = "1.0"

dashmap = "5.5"

```
tower-http = { version = "0.5.0", features = ["trace"] }

tracing = "0.1"

tracing-subscriber = { version = "0.3", features = ["env-filter"] }
```

Initialize the Logger and Add the Layer
In our `main` function, we first need to initialize the `tracing_subscriber`. Then, we can add the `TraceLayer` to our `Router` as a new layer. Layers are applied to all routes defined *after* the layer is added.

```
use axum::{routing::{get, post}, Router};
use dashmap::DashMap;
use std::sync::Arc;
use std::net::SocketAddr;
use tokio::net::TcpListener;
use tower_http::trace::TraceLayer;
use tracing_subscriber::{layer::SubscriberExt,
util::SubscriberInitExt};

// ... (keep the AppState, handlers, etc. from the previous section)

#[tokio::main]
async fn main() {
    // Initialize the tracing subscriber.
    // This will log events to the console.
    tracing_subscriber::registry()
        .with(
            tracing_subscriber::EnvFilter::try_from_default_env()
                .unwrap_or_else(|_|
"kv_store=debug,tower_http=debug".into()),
        )
        .with(tracing_subscriber::fmt::layer())
        .init();
```

```rust
    let shared_state = AppState::new(DashMap::new());

    // Add the TraceLayer as a middleware.
    let app = Router::new()
        .route("/", get(root_handler))
        .route("/keys", post(create_key))
        .route("/keys/:key", get(get_key))
        // The TraceLayer will log all requests and responses.
        .layer(TraceLayer::new_for_http())
        .with_state(shared_state);

    let addr = SocketAddr::from(([127, 0, 0, 1], 3000));
    tracing::debug!("Server listening on http://{}", addr); // Use tracing for logs
    let listener = TcpListener::bind(addr).await.unwrap();
    axum::serve(listener, app).await.unwrap();
}

// ... (rest of the handlers)
```

Now, when you run your server and make requests (e.g., `curl http://127.0.0.1:3000/keys/foo`), you will see detailed logs in your console for each request, including the method, path, status code, and latency. This is incredibly useful for debugging.

Writing Custom Middleware: Simple Authentication

What if we want to protect certain routes so they can only be accessed by clients who provide a valid authentication token? This requires custom logic, so we'll write our own middleware.

An Axum middleware is an `async` function that receives the `Request` and a special `Next` object. The middleware can run its logic, and then it calls `next.run(request)` to pass control to the next layer or to the final handler.

Let's create a simple authentication middleware that checks for the presence of a specific HTTP header: `X-Auth-Token: our-secret-token`.

```rust
use axum::{
    extract::Request,
    http::{header, StatusCode},
    middleware::{self, Next},
    response::Response,
};

async fn auth_middleware(req: Request, next: Next) -> Result<Response, StatusCode> {
    // Get the value of the `X-Auth-Token` header.
    let auth_token = req.headers()
        .get("X-Auth-Token")
        .and_then(|header| header.to_str().ok());

    // Check if the token is the one we expect.
    match auth_token {
        Some(token) if token == "our-secret-token" => {
            // Token is valid, so we pass the request to the next middleware or handler.
            Ok(next.run(req).await)
        }
```

```
    _ => {
        // Token is missing or invalid, so we return a 401 Unauthorized error.
        Err(StatusCode::UNAUTHORIZED)
    }
  }
}
```

Now, how do we apply this middleware? We don't want to protect every route, just the ones that modify data. Let's protect our POST /keys route. We can use `route_layer` to apply middleware to a single route.

```
// Inside main()

// The routes that do NOT require authentication.
let public_routes = Router::new()
    .route("/", get(root_handler))
    .route("/keys/:key", get(get_key));

// The routes that DO require authentication.
let protected_routes = Router::new()
    .route("/keys", post(create_key))
    // Apply our custom authentication middleware to this router.
    .route_layer(middleware::from_fn(auth_middleware));

// Combine the routers.
let app = Router::new()
    .merge(public_routes)
    .merge(protected_routes)
    .layer(TraceLayer::new_for_http())
    .with_state(shared_state);
```

With this setup, GET requests will work for anyone, but trying to POST a new key without the correct token will fail.

You can test this with `curl`:

This request will fail (401 Unauthorized):

```
curl -X POST http://127.0.0.1:3000/keys \ -H "Content-Type: application/json" \ -d '{"key": "mykey", "value": "myvalue"}'
```

This request will succeed (201 Created):

```
curl -X POST http://127.0.0.1:3000/keys \ -H "Content-Type: application/json" \ -H "X-Auth-Token: our-secret-token" \ -d '{"key": "mykey", "value": "myvalue"}'
```

Middleware is a cornerstone of modern web frameworks. It allows you to build a clean, layered architecture, keeping your handlers focused on business logic while delegating cross-cutting concerns like logging, authentication, and error handling to reusable, composable middleware components.

Performance Tuning and Benchmarking

Our web service is now feature-complete according to our initial plan. It's functional, handles concurrent requests, and has logging and authentication. But is it fast? How does it behave under heavy load?

Answering these questions is the domain of **performance tuning**. The cardinal rule of tuning is: **You can't improve what you don't measure.** Running your application on your local machine and subjectively feeling that it's "fast" is not a substitute for rigorous, repeatable measurements. **Benchmarking** is the process of putting your application under a controlled, heavy load to gather these measurements.

Choosing Your Benchmarking Tool

To benchmark a web server, you need a tool that can generate thousands of concurrent HTTP requests and measure the results. While many options exist, two excellent, easy-to-use choices are:

- **wrk**: A highly popular, fast, and scriptable command-line HTTP benchmarking tool. It's known for its ability to generate massive load from a single machine.
- **oha**: A modern, Rust-based alternative to `wrk` that provides beautiful, detailed terminal graphs and statistics, making it very user-friendly.

For our examples, we will use `oha` because its output is very clear, but the principles apply to any similar tool. You can install `oha` via `cargo`: `cargo install oha`.

Running Your First Benchmark

Let's start by measuring the performance of our `GET /keys/:key` endpoint. This is a read operation, and we expect it to be very fast.

First, run your `kv-store` server in a separate terminal. For a realistic benchmark, you should compile it in release mode, which applies many performance optimizations:

```
cargo run --release
```

Next, let's use `curl` to add a key to our store so we have something to read.

```
curl -X POST http://127.0.0.1:3000/keys \
 -H "Content-Type: application/json" \
 -H "X-Auth-Token: our-secret-token" \
 -d '{"key": "testkey", "value": "this is a test"}'
```

Now, in another terminal, we can run `oha` against the GET endpoint. Let's simulate 100 concurrent clients making requests for 10 seconds.

```
oha -c 100 -d 10s http://127.0.0.1:3000/keys/testkey
```

- `-c 100`: Use 100 concurrent clients.

- `-d 10s`: Run the test for a duration of 10 seconds.

`oha` will run and then present a detailed summary.

Interpreting the Results

The output from `oha` will look something like this (your numbers will vary):

Summary:

Success rate: 100.00%

Total: 10.00s

Slowest: 15.33ms

Fastest: 0.51ms

Average: 2.13ms

Requests/sec: 46891.23

Latency distribution:

10% in 0.95ms

25% in 1.43ms

50% in 2.01ms

75% in 2.65ms

90% in 3.41ms

95% in 4.12ms

99% in 6.78ms

What should you look for?

- **Requests/sec (RPS)**: This is your **throughput**. It's the primary measure of your server's capacity. Higher is better.
- **Average Latency**: The average time it took to serve a request. Lower is better.
- **Latency Distribution (Percentiles)**: This is often more important than the average. The `99%` value (p99 latency) tells you that 99% of requests were faster than this number. A low p99 latency indicates that your server is consistently fast, even for the slowest requests. A high p99, even with a good average, can indicate performance problems under load.

Identifying and Fixing a Bottleneck: The Case of Logging

Let's imagine our benchmark results are lower than we expect. Where do we look for problems? One of the first places to investigate in a new application is logging.

Our current setup uses `tower_http::trace::TraceLayer`, which is fantastic for development. It logs every single request and response. However, writing to the console (or a file) is a relatively slow I/O operation. Under heavy load, the logging itself can become a bottleneck, slowing down the server.

A common practice is to have different logging levels for development and production. In production, you might only log errors or warnings, not every single `DEBUG` or `TRACE` level event.

The Fix: Let's adjust our `main.rs` to have a less verbose logging configuration when not in `DEBUG` mode. We can use the `RUST_LOG` environment variable to control this.

```
// Inside main()

tracing_subscriber::registry()

  .with(

    tracing_subscriber::EnvFilter::try_from_default_env()

      // A more sensible production default: log our app's info messages

      // and warnings or errors from all other crates.

      .unwrap_or_else(|_| "kv_store=info,warn".into()),

  )

  .with(tracing_subscriber::fmt::layer())

  .init()
```

With this change, if `RUST_LOG` is not set, it defaults to a much quieter setting. The noisy `tower_http` debug logs will no longer be processed or written, reducing overhead.

Benchmarking Again

After making this change, we would compile in release mode and run the exact same `oha` command again.

```
# First, recompile with the change
cargo build --release
# Then run the server
./target/release/kv-store

# In another terminal, run the benchmark again
oha -c 100 -d 10s http://127.0.0.1:3000/keys/testkey
```

You would very likely see an improvement in both throughput (Requests/sec) and latency, especially the p99 latency. This iterative cycle—**measure, identify, fix, measure again**—is the core loop of performance tuning. It transforms performance work from guesswork into a scientific process, allowing you to systematically find and eliminate bottlenecks to make your application as fast and efficient as possible.

Chapter 6:
Testing, Debugging, and Deploying Async Rust

We have successfully designed and built a complete, concurrent web service. But our work as software engineers isn't finished when the feature is built; we must also ensure it is correct, robust, and reliable. This final chapter is dedicated to the essential practices that take an application from a "works on my machine" prototype to a production-ready system.

We will cover strategies for testing concurrent code, techniques for debugging complex async interactions, and best practices for packaging and deploying your application for the world to use. We'll begin with the foundation of software quality: testing.

Strategies for Testing Async Code

Testing synchronous code is straightforward. You call a function with some input and assert that the output is what you expect. Testing asynchronous code follows the same principle, but with one key difference: the tests themselves need to be executed within an async runtime. A standard `#[test]` function is synchronous; it has no way to `.await` a `Future`.

Fortunately, the Tokio ecosystem provides excellent tools to make testing async code feel just as natural as testing synchronous code.

Unit Testing with `#[tokio::test]`

For testing a single, isolated piece of async logic—a **unit test**—the `#[tokio::test]` macro is your primary tool. Much like `#[tokio::main]`, this macro transforms a standard test function into an `async fn` and wraps it in a small, single-threaded Tokio runtime instance created just for that test.

Let's write a unit test for a simple async function that adds two numbers after a short delay.

```rust
use tokio::time::{self, Duration};

// The async function we want to test.
async fn add_async(a: u32, b: u32) -> u32 {
    time::sleep(Duration::from_millis(10)).await;
    a + b
}

// To use `#[tokio::test]`, you need to enable the "macros" feature for tokio
// in your `Cargo.toml` dev-dependencies section.
// [dev-dependencies]
// tokio = { version = "1", features = ["macros"] }

#[cfg(test)]
mod tests {
    use super::*;

    #[tokio::test]
    async fn test_add_async() {
        // Inside this function, we can use .await.
        let result = add_async(5, 10).await;
        assert_eq!(result, 15);
    }
}
```

This looks and feels just like a regular test, which is the goal. The `#[tokio::test]` macro handles the boilerplate of setting up and tearing down a runtime for you, allowing you to focus on the test's logic.

Testing More Complex Logic

You can use this same pattern to test more complex components that use other async primitives. For example, let's test a small actor that manages a counter. We can send it commands and then check its state, all within a single test.

use tokio::sync::{mpsc, oneshot};

```rust
// The actor and commands from our earlier chapter.
struct CounterActor {
    receiver: mpsc::Receiver<CounterCommand>,
    counter: i32,
}
enum CounterCommand {
    Increment,
    GetValue { responder: oneshot::Sender<i32> },
}
impl CounterActor {
    fn new(receiver: mpsc::Receiver<CounterCommand>) -> Self {
        Self { receiver, counter: 0 }
    }
    async fn run(&mut self) {
        while let Some(command) = self.receiver.recv().await {
            match command {
                CounterCommand::Increment => self.counter += 1,
                CounterCommand::GetValue { responder } => {
                    let _ = responder.send(self.counter);
                }
            }
        }
    }
}

#[cfg(test)]
mod actor_tests {
    use super::*;
    use tokio::time::Duration;
```

```
#[tokio::test]
async fn test_counter_actor() {
    let (tx, rx) = mpsc::channel(10);
    let mut actor = CounterActor::new(rx);

    // Spawn the actor to run in the background for our test.
    tokio::spawn(async move { actor.run().await });

    // Send a few commands.
    tx.send(CounterCommand::Increment).await.unwrap();
    tx.send(CounterCommand::Increment).await.unwrap();

    // Send a request to get the value.
    let (resp_tx, resp_rx) = oneshot::channel();
    tx.send(CounterCommand::GetValue { responder: resp_tx
}).await.unwrap();

    // Await the response and assert it's correct.
    let final_value = resp_rx.await.unwrap();
    assert_eq!(final_value, 2);
  }
}
```

Integration Testing for Your Web Service

While unit tests are great for isolated logic, **integration tests** are for verifying that multiple components of your application work together correctly. For our `kv-store` service, we want to write a test that simulates real HTTP requests and verifies the behavior of our entire Axum router, its handlers, and the shared state.

A naive approach would be to run the server in one thread and have a separate test client connect to it over a real TCP port. This is possible, but it's slow and brittle. A better way is to test the `Router` directly in memory. Since our Axum `app` is a `tower::Service`, we can pass a mocked `Request` to it and get a `Response` back without ever touching the network.

Let's write an integration test for our key-value store. This test will live in the `tests/` directory of our project, which is Rust's convention for integration tests.

Create a file `tests/kv_store.rs`:

// This requires adding axum, tokio, etc. to [dev-dependencies] in Cargo.toml

// We need to import the functions and types from our main binary crate.

use kv_store::{create_key, get_key, AppState, CreatePayload}; // Assuming these are public in lib.rs or main.rs

use axum::{

  body::Body,

  http::{self, Request, StatusCode},

  Router,

};

use dashmap::DashMap;

use http_body_util::BodyExt; // for .to_bytes()

use serde_json::json;

use std::sync::Arc;

use tower::ServiceExt; // for `oneshot`

// A helper function to build our app router for tests.

fn test_app() -> Router {

```rust
    let shared_state = AppState::new(DashMap::new());
    Router::new()
        .route("/keys", axum::routing::post(create_key))
        .route("/keys/:key", axum::routing::get(get_key))
        .with_state(shared_state)
}

#[tokio::test]
async fn test_create_and_get_key() {
    let app = test_app();

    // -- Test POST /keys --
    let post_request = Request::builder()
        .method(http::Method::POST)
        .uri("/keys")
        .header(http::header::CONTENT_TYPE, "application/json")
        .body(Body::from(
            json!({
                "key": "test-key",
                "value": "test-value"
```

```rust
        }).to_string(),
    ))
    .unwrap();

    // Drive the request through the app service.
    let post_response = app.clone().oneshot(post_request).await.unwrap();

    assert_eq!(post_response.status(), StatusCode::CREATED);

    // -- Test GET /keys/:key --
    let get_request = Request::builder()
        .uri("/keys/test-key")
        .body(Body::empty())
        .unwrap();

    let get_response = app.oneshot(get_request).await.unwrap();

    assert_eq!(get_response.status(), StatusCode::OK);

    // Assert on the response body.
    let body = get_response.into_body().collect().await.unwrap().to_bytes();

    let body_as_string: String = serde_json::from_slice(&body).unwrap();

    assert_eq!(body_as_string, "test-value");
}
```

```rust
#[tokio::test]
async fn test_get_nonexistent_key() {
    let app = test_app();
    let request = Request::builder()
        .uri("/keys/nonexistent-key")
        .body(Body::empty())
        .unwrap();
    let response = app.oneshot(request).await.unwrap();
    assert_eq!(response.status(), StatusCode::NOT_FOUND);
}
```

This in-memory testing approach is extremely fast and reliable. It allows you to write comprehensive tests for your entire API surface—validating success cases, error cases, status codes, and response bodies—all without the overhead and flakiness of real network requests.

Common Debugging Scenarios: Gaining Visibility with tracing

When an application behaves unexpectedly, our first instinct is often to sprinkle `println!` statements throughout the code to see the flow of execution and the state of variables. This works reasonably well for simple, sequential programs.

However, in a concurrent application like our web server, `println!` quickly becomes a liability. With hundreds of requests being handled in parallel, your console output turns into an unreadable, interleaved mess of messages. It's nearly impossible to follow the lifecycle of a single request from start to finish. You're left asking questions like, "Which `get_key` call does this `value found` message belong to?"

To solve this, we need a way to produce structured, context-aware diagnostic information. This is precisely what the **tracing** crate and its ecosystem are designed for. `tracing` is a framework for instrumenting applications to collect timed, structured, and context-rich diagnostic data.

The Core Concepts of `tracing`

`tracing` introduces two fundamental concepts that replace traditional log messages:

1. **Event**: An `event` is a point-in-time notification. It's the `tracing` equivalent of a log line. You can create events at different levels (e.g., `error!`, `warn!`, `info!`, `debug!`, `trace!`) and attach key-value data to them.
2. **Span**: A `span` represents a period of time with a beginning and an end. This is the feature that provides the crucial context that `println!` lacks. A span has a name, and you can associate data with it. When a task "enters" a span, all events that occur within that task are understood to be happening *inside* that span. Spans can be nested, creating a clear, hierarchical view of your program's execution.

A **Subscriber** is the component (from `tracing-subscriber`) that collects, filters, and processes all the event and span data emitted by your application. We've already initialized a basic one in our middleware section; now, let's explore how to leverage it for debugging.

Instrumenting Your Code for Better Visibility

The easiest and most powerful way to use `tracing` is with the `#[tracing::instrument]` attribute macro. You can attach this to your functions to automatically create a span every time that function is called.

The span will automatically be named after the function, and critically, it will record the function's arguments as key-value data. Let's apply this to our `kv-store` handlers to see it in action.

```rust
use axum::{
    extract::{Path, State},
    http::StatusCode,
    response::IntoResponse,
    Json,
};
use serde::Deserialize;

// GET /keys/:key
// This handler retrieves a value for a given key.
#[tracing::instrument(skip(state))] // We skip `state` because it's large and not useful to log.
async fn get_key(
    State(state): State<AppState>,
    Path(key): Path<String>,
) -> impl IntoResponse {
    tracing::info!("Attempting to retrieve value for key.");
    if let Some(value_ref) = state.get(&key) {
        let value = value_ref.clone();
        tracing::debug!("Key found. Returning value.");
        (StatusCode::OK, Json(value))
    } else {
        tracing::warn!("Key not found.");
        (StatusCode::NOT_FOUND, Json("Key not found".to_string()))
    }
}
```

```rust
#[derive(Deserialize)]
struct CreatePayload {
    key: String,
    value: String,
}

// POST /keys
// This handler sets a new key-value pair.
#[tracing::instrument(skip(state))]
async fn create_key(
    State(state): State<AppState>,
    Json(payload): Json<CreatePayload>,
) -> impl IntoResponse {
    tracing::info!("Attempting to create a new key-value pair.");
    state.insert(payload.key, payload.value);
    StatusCode::CREATED
}
// Remember to update the router in main() to use these instrumented handlers.
```

- `#[tracing::instrument]` automatically creates a span when `get_key` or `create_key` is called.
- The span's data will include the arguments. For `get_key`, it will log `key = "some-value"`.
- We use `skip(state)` to tell `tracing` not to try and record the entire `AppState`, as this is not practical.
- Inside the function, we use `tracing::info!`, `debug!`, and `warn!` to emit events.

Reading the Structured Output

Now, with the `TraceLayer` middleware and our instrumented handlers, let's make a request and examine the console output.

```
curl http://127.0.0.1:3000/keys/my-test-key
```

The output will look fundamentally different from a series of `println!`s. It will be structured and contextual (the exact format depends on your subscriber settings):

```
DEBUG tower_http::trace::on_request: request
  method=GET
  uri=/keys/my-test-key
  version=HTTP/1.1
  headers={...}

INFO kv_store::get_key: get_key
  key="my-test-key"
  message="Attempting to retrieve value for key."

WARN kv_store::get_key: get_key
  key="my-test-key"
  message="Key not found."

DEBUG tower_http::trace::on_response: response
  latency=257.µs
  status=404
  headers={...}
```

This output is far more valuable:

1. **Context is Preserved**: We can clearly see that the "Attempting to retrieve..." and "Key not found" events belong to the `get_key` span, which was called with `key="my-test-key"`.
2. **Hierarchy is Clear**: The `tower_http` spans wrap our handler's span, showing the full lifecycle of the request, from the moment it was received to the moment the response was sent, including the final status code and latency.
3. **It's Searchable**: This structured log format is machine-readable. You can feed it into logging platforms (like

Datadog, Splunk, or the ELK stack) and easily search for all events related to a specific key, a specific user ID, or a specific request trace.

By adopting `tracing`, you move from debugging with a simple flashlight to observing your application with a detailed schematic diagram. It provides the visibility and context necessary to understand, debug, and maintain complex, concurrent systems effectively.

Packaging Your Application for Production Using Docker

We've built, tested, and benchmarked our application. It runs perfectly on our local machine. The final step before deployment is to package it in a way that is portable, reproducible, and secure. We need to ensure that the application we run in production is identical to the one we tested, regardless of the server's operating system or pre-installed software.

The industry-standard solution for this is **containerization**, and the most popular tool for containerization is **Docker**.

Why Use Containers?

A container is a lightweight, standalone, executable package of software that includes everything needed to run it: the code, a runtime, system tools, system libraries, and settings. It bundles the application and its environment together.

This solves the classic "it works on my machine" problem. By packaging our `kv-store` service into a Docker container, we create a single "artifact" that can be run anywhere Docker is installed—on a developer's laptop, a testing server, or in a cloud environment like AWS or Google Cloud—with the guarantee that it will behave identically in every environment.

The Dockerfile: A Blueprint for Your Application

You define a Docker container using a special text file called a `Dockerfile`. This file contains a series of step-by-step instructions that Docker follows to build a container **image**. An image is a read-only template that contains your application and its dependencies. You can then run one or more **containers** from that single image.

For a compiled language like Rust, the best practice is to use a **multi-stage build**. This is a powerful technique that allows us to use a large, feature-rich container for compiling our code, and then copy *only* the final, compiled binary into a tiny, clean, and secure container for production. This results in significantly smaller and more secure production images.

Let's write a `Dockerfile` for our `kv-store` service. Create a new file named `Dockerfile` in the root of your project directory.

```dockerfile
# --- Stage 1: The Builder ---
# We start with the official Rust image, which contains the full Rust toolchain.
# We give this stage a name, "builder", so we can refer to it later.
FROM rust:1.78 as builder

# Set the working directory inside the container.
WORKDIR /usr/src/kv-store

# Copy the Cargo manifest files.
# This is done as a separate step to leverage Docker's layer caching.
# If these files don't change, Docker won't re-download dependencies.
COPY Cargo.toml Cargo.lock ./

# Build a dummy project to cache dependencies.
```

```dockerfile
# This creates a `target` directory with our dependencies
compiled.
RUN mkdir src && \
    echo "fn main() {}" > src/main.rs && \
    cargo build --release && \
    rm -rf src

# Now, copy our actual application source code.
COPY . .

# Build our application for release.
# This will be much faster because dependencies are already
cached.
RUN cargo build --release

# --- Stage 2: The Final Image ---
# We start from a minimal base image. `debian:bullseye-slim` is small
# and includes basic necessities like SSL certificates.
FROM debian:bullseye-slim

# Copy the compiled binary from the "builder" stage.
# The binary is located at /usr/src/kv-store/target/release/kv-store.
COPY --from=builder /usr/src/kv-store/target/release/kv-store /usr/local/bin/kv-store

# Set the command to run when the container starts.
# This executes our application binary.
CMD ["/usr/local/bin/kv-store"]
```

Understanding the Multi-Stage Build

Let's break down this `Dockerfile`:

Stage 1: The `builder`

- **`FROM rust:1.78 as builder`**: We start with the official Rust image, which is large because it contains the

compiler, `cargo`, and all build dependencies. We name this stage `builder`.
- **WORKDIR /usr/src/kv-store**: This sets the current directory for subsequent commands.
- **COPY Cargo.toml Cargo.lock ./ and RUN cargo build --release**: This is a key optimization. We copy only the manifest files first and then run a build. Docker caches the result of each step (a "layer"). If we later change our source code but not our dependencies, Docker can reuse the cached layer with all our compiled dependencies, making subsequent builds much faster.
- **COPY . .**: Now we copy our application's source code (`src/main.rs`, etc.).
- **RUN cargo build --release**: We build our actual application. This step will use the cached dependencies and only needs to compile our own code, making it very quick. The final, optimized binary will be located at `/usr/src/kv-store/target/release/kv-store`.

Stage 2: The Final Image
- **FROM debian:bullseye-slim**: This is the start of our final production image. We use a very small, general-purpose base image. Everything from the `builder` stage is discarded, except for what we explicitly copy over.
- **COPY --from=builder ...**: This is the magic of a multi-stage build. We copy *only* the compiled application binary from the `builder` stage into our new, clean image. We place it in `/usr/local/bin/` which is a standard location for user-installed executables.
- **CMD ["/usr/local/bin/kv-store"]**: This specifies the default command to execute when a container is started from this image. It simply runs our application.

Building and Running Your Container

With the `Dockerfile` in place, you can now build and run your application using the Docker CLI.

1. Build the Image

From your project's root directory, run the `docker build` command. We'll give our image a name (`kv-store-app`) and a version tag (`v1`).

```
docker build -t kv-store-app:v1 .
```

The `.` at the end tells Docker to look for the `Dockerfile` in the current directory.

2. Run the Container

Once the build is complete, you can start a container from your new image using `docker run`.

```
docker run -p 3000:3000 --rm --name my-kv-store kv-store-app:v1
```

Let's break down these flags:
- `-p 3000:3000`: This maps a port from your host machine to the container. It connects port `3000` on your local machine to port `3000` inside the container (where our Axum server is listening).
- `--rm`: This is a convenience flag that automatically removes the container when it exits.
- `--name my-kv-store`: This gives your running container a human-readable name.
- `kv-store-app:v1`: This is the name and tag of the image you want to run.

Your server is now running inside a container! You can interact with it using `curl` from your host machine exactly as before: `curl http://127.0.0.1:3000`.

By following this process, you have created a portable, efficient, and secure package for your application, ready to be deployed to any modern cloud or server environment.

Adding Monitoring and Observability with Prometheus Metrics

Our application is packaged and ready for the world. But once it's deployed, how do we know if it's healthy? `tracing` gives us detailed logs to debug specific problems, but it doesn't give us a high-level, real-time overview of the system's performance and behavior.

This is the role of **monitoring and observability**. We need to collect quantitative data—or **metrics**—about our application's performance over time. This data allows us to build dashboards, set up automated alerts, and understand performance trends.

Key questions we might want to answer include:

- How many requests per second is the server handling right now?
- What is the p99 latency for our `POST /keys` endpoint over the last hour?
- How many active database connections do we have?
- Is our application's memory usage growing over time?

The standard tool for collecting and storing this kind of time-series data in the cloud-native world is **Prometheus**.

The Prometheus Model: Scraping Metrics

Prometheus works on a "pull" or "scrape" model. Your application doesn't push metrics to a central server. Instead, your application exposes a simple HTTP endpoint (usually `/metrics`) that displays all its current metrics in a text-based format. The Prometheus server is configured to periodically connect to this endpoint, "scrape" the current values, and store them in its time-series database.

This approach is simple, robust, and decouples your application from the monitoring system.

Instrumenting Our Application

To expose Prometheus metrics, we need to instrument our code. We'll use two key crates:

- **metrics**: A facade that provides a simple API for creating and updating metrics (counters, gauges, histograms).
- **metrics-exporter-prometheus**: A library that hooks into the `metrics` facade and provides the functionality to render the metrics in the Prometheus format and serve them over HTTP.

1. Add Dependencies

Update your `Cargo.toml` with the new dependencies.

```toml
[dependencies]

# ... existing dependencies

metrics = "0.22"

metrics-exporter-prometheus = "0.13"
```

2. Create and Install the Prometheus Recorder

In our main function, we need to set up the Prometheus "recorder." This recorder will listen on a separate port to serve the /metrics endpoint. We then install it as the global metrics collector for our application.

```rust
// In main.rs
use metrics_exporter_prometheus::{PrometheusBuilder, PrometheusHandle};

// A helper function to set up the metrics endpoint.
fn setup_metrics() -> PrometheusHandle {
    const METRICS_PORT: u16 = 9000;
```

```
    let metrics_addr = SocketAddr::from(([127, 0, 0, 1],
METRICS_PORT));
    tracing::debug!("Metrics server listening on http://{}",
metrics_addr);

    PrometheusBuilder::new()
        .with_http_listener(metrics_addr)
        .install_recorder()
        .unwrap()
}
// Inside main()
#[tokio::main]
async fn main() {
    // ... tracing setup ...
    let _metrics_handle = setup_metrics(); // Set up the /metrics
endpoint.
    // ... rest of the main function ...
}
```

Instrumenting Our Code with Metrics

Now, we can use the macros from the `metrics` crate to record data. Let's add some useful metrics to our handlers.

- **`counter!`**: An always-increasing value. Perfect for tracking total requests.
- **`gauge!`**: A value that can go up and down. Good for tracking things like active connections.
- **`histogram!`**: Tracks the distribution of a set of values. This is ideal for measuring request latency.

Let's instrument our `create_key` handler.

```
use metrics::{counter, histogram};

use std::time::Instant;

#[tracing::instrument(skip(state))]
```

```rust
async fn create_key(
    State(state): State<AppState>,
    Json(payload): Json<CreatePayload>,
) -> impl IntoResponse {
    let start = Instant::now();
    tracing::info!("Attempting to create a new key-value pair.");
    state.insert(payload.key.clone(), payload.value);
    // Record metrics for this operation.
    // 1. Increment a counter for the total number of requests to this endpoint.
    counter!("requests_total", "endpoint" => "POST /keys").increment(1);
    // 2. Record the latency of this operation in a histogram.
    let duration = start.elapsed().as_secs_f64();
    histogram!("request_latency_seconds", "endpoint" => "POST /keys").record(duration);
    StatusCode::CREATED
}
```

Notice the labels like `"endpoint" => "POST /keys"`. These allow you to slice and dice your data in Prometheus. You can get the total number of requests across all endpoints, or just for a specific one.

We can also use a middleware to automatically record metrics for all routes.

```rust
use axum::{extract::Request, http::StatusCode,
middleware::Next, response::Response};
use std::time::Instant;

async fn metrics_middleware(req: Request, next: Next) ->
Response {
    let start = Instant::now();
    // Get the path to use as a label.
    let path = req.uri().path().to_owned();
    let method = req.method().clone();

    // Run the next middleware or handler.
    let response = next.run(req).await;

    let latency = start.elapsed().as_secs_f64();
    let status = response.status().as_u16().to_string();

    // Create a metric with labels.
    let labels = [
        ("method", method.to_string()),
        ("path", path),
        ("status", status),
    ];

    counter!("http_requests_total", &labels).increment(1);
    histogram!("http_requests_latency_seconds",
&labels).record(latency);

    response
}

// In main(), apply this as a middleware layer to your router.
let app = Router::new()
    // ... your routes ...
    .route_layer(middleware::from_fn(metrics_middleware))
    // ... other layers ...
```

```
.with_state(shared_state);
```

Scraping and Viewing the Metrics

With the application instrumented and running, you can now see the metrics it's producing.

1. **Run your kv-store server**: `cargo run --release`
2. **Access the metrics endpoint**: In a browser or with `curl`, go to `http://127.0.0.1:9000/metrics`. You will see output in the Prometheus text format:

```
# HELP http_requests_total Number of HTTP requests received.
# TYPE http_requests_total counter
http_requests_total{method="POST",path="/keys",status="201"} 1
# HELP http_requests_latency_seconds HTTP request latency in seconds.
# TYPE http_requests_latency_seconds histogram
http_requests_latency_seconds_bucket{method="POST",path="/keys",status="201",le="0.005"} 1
...
```

To make this data useful, you would run a Prometheus server and configure it to "scrape" this endpoint every 15 or 30 seconds. In Prometheus's query interface, you could then run queries like:

- `rate(http_requests_total{job="kv-store"}[5m])`: To see the requests-per-second rate over the last 5 minutes.
- `histogram_quantile(0.99, sum(rate(http_requests_latency_seconds_bucket{job="kv-store"}[5m])) by (le))`: To calculate the p99 latency.

By instrumenting your application with metrics, you gain a powerful, quantitative understanding of its health and performance. This is no longer a "nice-to-have"; for any service running in production, it is an essential part of the operational toolkit.

A Look Toward the Future of Asynchronous Rust

Throughout this book, we have journeyed from the fundamental "why" of asynchronous programming to building a complete, production-ready web service. We've wrangled futures, managed state, and handled concurrency with the powerful tools that the Rust ecosystem provides today. But the journey of a language and its ecosystem is never over.

The async story in Rust is still being written. The foundations are incredibly strong, but the community and language team are constantly working to make it even more powerful, ergonomic, and accessible. In this final section, we'll take a look at the horizon and explore some of the exciting developments that are shaping the future of async Rust.

The Path to Polish: `async fn` *in Traits*

One of the most anticipated features in the async ecosystem is the stabilization of using `async fn` directly in traits. Today, if you want to define a trait where implementers must provide an asynchronous method, you have to use workarounds involving macros like `#[async_trait]`.

While `async_trait` is a brilliant and widely-used library, its approach has some performance and ergonomic trade-offs. The language team is actively working on building this capability directly into the compiler.

When this feature is fully stabilized, defining an asynchronous trait will look as natural as this:

```
// A potential future syntax

trait MessageProcessor {
```

```rust
// This would just work, without any helper macros.
async fn process_message(&self, message: &str) -> Result<(), std::io::Error>;
}
```

This seemingly small change will have a huge impact. It will make writing generic, abstract async libraries cleaner and more performant, removing a significant hurdle for developers and solidifying `async` as a first-class, fully integrated citizen of the language.

Peering into the Engine: Better Tooling and Debuggability

As we've seen, debugging concurrent systems can be challenging. While `tracing` gives us fantastic visibility, the community is pushing for even more powerful, purpose-built tools.

The `tokio-console` project is a prime example of this future direction. It's a debugging and diagnostics tool specifically for async Rust applications. Instead of just showing text logs, it provides a live, interactive terminal UI that gives you a high-level overview of your entire application's async operations. You can see:

- A list of all running tasks and how long they've been busy.
- Which tasks are currently waiting on I/O and which are waiting on locks.
- How much time each task spends being polled versus being idle.
- Warnings about common performance issues, like tasks that are blocking the executor.

The continued development of `tokio-console` and other tools like it will fundamentally change how we debug async Rust. It moves us from analyzing a textual representation of the past to observing the live, dynamic behavior of the system as a whole, making it much easier to spot bottlenecks, deadlocks, and other hard-to-find concurrent bugs.

New Frontiers: Specialized Runtimes and `io_uring`

Tokio is a phenomenal general-purpose runtime, but the future will likely see the rise of more specialized runtimes tailored for specific environments.

- **Embedded and WebAssembly (Wasm)**: The need for non-blocking I/O is just as critical in resource-constrained embedded systems and in browser-based Wasm applications. We are seeing the growth of smaller, more focused runtimes designed to work efficiently in these environments where binary size and memory usage are paramount.
- `io_uring`: On Linux, `io_uring` is a revolutionary new system for asynchronous I/O that is even more efficient than the `epoll` system that Tokio currently uses. It allows for true, kernel-level asynchronous operations for both networking and file I/O, reducing syscall overhead and improving performance. As `io_uring` matures, we can expect to see runtimes (or versions of Tokio) that are built on top of it, unlocking another level of performance for I/O-intensive applications on Linux.

The Road Ahead is Bright

The asynchronous ecosystem in Rust is one of the most vibrant and rapidly innovating areas of the language. Driven by a dedicated community and a clear focus on performance and safety, the tools and patterns we have today are already world-class. The developments on the horizon promise to make them even better.

By learning the principles in this book, you have built a solid foundation on a technology that is designed for the future. You are now well-equipped not only to build high-performance, concurrent systems today but also to grow and adapt alongside the exciting evolution of asynchronous Rust tomorrow.

Made in the USA
Columbia, SC
02 July 2025